The New Brass Ring

DMADD, Process Improvement
for the 21st Century

Phillip C. Reinke

Eloquent Books

Eloquent Books
An imprint of Strategic Book Group
P.O. Box 333
Durham CT 06422
www.StrategicBookGroup.com

ISBN: 978-1-60911-613-2

Printed in the United States of America

Book Design: Rolando F. Santos

Contents

Dedication

To those who asked
"Why not?"
and took the initiative to answer that question.

To my wife, Lori. Need I say
more?

Preface

"If I have seen further, it is by standing on the shoulders of giants."
—*Sir Isaac Newton*

"What has been is what will be, and what has been done is what will be done; there is nothing new under the sun."
—*Ecclesiastes 1:9*

THE latest downturn in the economy has emphasized what I call the "Strive to Thrive" organizational cycle. The 21st century, from an organizational perspective, is a merry-go-round. Not only does a business go round and round, but it also has its ups and downs during its journey. It is a set of nested cycles. Now more than ever, the ride is filled to capacity, with each of the riders reaching for one of the many brass rings that dangle just out of reach.

"Brass rings?" you ask.

On the traditional carousel rides, a brass ring was placed on a hook. It was not within easy reach. Grabbing the ring got that person another ride. It provided a form of entertainment for the ride's passengers during a rather boring circle. Capturing one of those rings was the coveted prize. It brings with its possession a "free ride" — and, sometimes, riches beyond one's wildest dreams.

Over the course of my career, I have been involved in numerous iterations of focused efforts in organizational and process improvement. Many were significantly successful, others not so successful. One thing that each had in common was that the efforts were not lasting. Each effort created a group of real practitioners and a horde of imitators. The horde brought a "bad name" to each successive effort and catalyzed its demise. The good news has been that the predecessor of each has been an improvement over the prior. There is a new brass ring dangling just out of reach. It is a "solution-driven," process improvement (PI) methodology that is well-suited to the 21st century.

If you are looking for an entirely new methodology, you will be disappointed. If you are looking for a continuous improvement management methodology (CIMM) compatible with the 21st century, which will set the stage for cost-effective problem solving, you may be delighted!

I do not purport to be an Ecclesiastical writer or Isaac Newton. I believe that what we are doing is a natural result of the age of information: a simple leveraging of the understated and unappreciated benefits of the 21st century. Even in the 1980s and 1990s, obtaining comprehensive information was difficult at best. The natural outcome of that climate was Six Sigma, a "discovery-based" problem-solving methodology. I have classified it as "discovery-based" in that it strives, through analytical means to discover the root causes of an issue and apply solutions that reduce the impact of the identified drivers. Simply stated, it is the manipulation of regression analysis—scientific method in its purest form! However, the competitive nature of the Internet has created a vast resource of information that is underutilized by those self-reliant and creative individuals who perform the continuous improvement function within organizations. A downside is that a narrow perspective often results in reinventing the wheel as a result of their self-imposed paradigms. In an academic sense, the "new PI order" is the literature search of a thesis or a dissertation and the application of the learning, taking the effort to higher and better levels.

My career has spanned from operations to industrial engineering and the use of Frederick Taylor's scientific management methodologies. It continued through participative management, through Philip Crosby's, Total Quality Management (TQM), Michael Hammer's re-engineering, and, finally, Mikel Harry's Six Sigma. I anxiously awaited the next evolution of process improvement and it did not appear. I have seen Six Sigma morphed and bastardized by fly-by-night consultants looking to make a buck. I have also dug deep into many of the variants aligned with Six Sigma to make it, as these "practitioners" claim, an "end-all" in process improvement. In all of the searching, I did not find a methodology that aligned itself with the benefits of the new millennium; those being, the myriad of solutions for existing problems, that reside on the internet, just waiting to be adapted and implemented. This is what solution-based problem solving is in a nutshell. So out of a combination of necessity and desire, I too morphed Six Sigma, leveraging its original strengths into what is called the "new PI order," or Define-Measure-Analyze-Develop-Deliver (DMADD).

DMADD was named so for numerous reasons. First, it looks like a Six Sigma discipline. For those who have not experienced with the Six Sigma process improvement methodology, it is a systematic discipline that clearly defines the problem and goals, creates relevant measures of success, analyzes the problem with representative data, improves the problem at the source of the issue and controls the improvement in way to ensure that it is sustained. The acronym commonly used by practitioners is DMAIC which stands for define, measure, analyze, improve and control. The Six Sigma methodology is performed by certified individuals called Greenbelts, Blackbelts or Master Blackbelts. DMAIC and DMADD should not be put into the same class. Although the acronyms look the same, DMAIC and DMADD set about providing solutions in very different ways.

When I first unveiled the new process improvement discipline, many years ago, the leaders of the organization balked at it. I simply changed the name and presented it again and it was quickly embraced! I realized that I could leverage the broad organizational acceptance of a Six Sigma lookalike acronym. This made organizational implementation more palatable and easier to digest. In reality, that is where most of the similarity to Six Sigma ends.

Second, it embeds existing solutions developed by past discoveries (many of them from Six Sigma) into the initial phases of the effort. A definite no-no in the Six Sigma arena, which refrains from entertaining preconceived solutions until the "improve" or

Philip C. Reinke

"I" phase of DMAIC.

I believe that DMADD is the next methodology that stands on the shoulders of the giants of the 20th century process improvement—Taylor, Shewhart, Deming, Crosby, Harry and others.

If you have been in process improvement for any length of time, you have experienced the following situations:

Having worked tirelessly for months on a DMAIC project. Then an old-timer announces to the organization that he/she has been recommending that for years and pulls out a file full of memos confirming it.

Hearing that the innovation solution that you implemented was already being used successfully in a sister division—or worse, a competitor.

Finding out that, after spending tens of thousands on a specialized process improvement activity called, "Triz," and the research, only to have the recommended fixes, quashed.

Process improvement has committed a cardinal sin by resting on its laurels and not continuing to reinvent itself. Some may argue that Lean-Six Sigma is the evolution. I contend that it simply adjusted to executive demands for faster results and broader application and, as a result, it compromised itself. Our bottom line is that if the current iteration of Six Sigma is meeting your organizational needs, continue on this track. If not, consider stepping into the Information Age with DMADD, the process improvement methodology of the 21st century.

x

Chapter 1

Enter the Club

EARLY in the history of humankind, a discovery arose from an interaction between two of our ancestors. Although the specific details will never be known, let's assume that an argument over food took place. In frustration, (it is postulated that patience is a more advanced human trait), one of the two picked up a branch and struck the other. The victim fell dead to the ground. From this simple interaction grew the weapon: the club. Although millennia have passed since its discovery, the club remains exactly as effective as it did on that first day.

The basic concept behind the club remains the same even though it has gone through many variations and improvements that — as gruesome as it seems— let you hit your opponent hard and often to wound or kill him. Improvements to the handle to make it more user-friendly, weight distribution to improve effectiveness and adornments make it scarier. Up until the past few centuries, the club remained the mainstay of killing and property destruction. Many wars were fought solely with clubs or their variants.

Fast-forward to the 21st century. The basic concept of warfare remains the same: Kill lots of people and do lots of damage. Although the basics of the club remain the same, the enhancements have leaped forward significantly. Soldiers no longer have to face each other and pound away. Killing can be accomplished at a distance, with unheard-of accuracy. In fact, opposing sides no longer even need to be involved. Advanced technology allows for one side to send machines in, to accomplish the work for them. Though the basic concept of the club is unchanged, it has just evolved from a manual/brute force tool, to a more precise, automated, and effective one. It advanced to a spear, then to an arrow and then to a bullet and then to a bomb and now a precision-guided missile. Yet the basic club concept remains and is still as effective as it was when it was first discovered.

In fact, in military training, the recruit is taught that if all advanced technology fails and/or runs out, they should depend upon hand-to-hand combat. The most effective method to use is (you guessed it) the club.

What does the club and warfare have to do with process improvement? Having been involved in process improvement from statistical process control (SPC) to Quality Circles to TQM to Re-engineering to Six Sigma, I have seen numerous enhancements to the process improvement methodology, yet I see the club and its many iterations!

Imagine a scenario in which after careful analysis, our military determined that the basic club is the most reliable and cost-effective weapon. As a result of this analysis, all other weapons (offensive and defensive) were mothballed and the entire force was outfitted with clubs. We do not have to be schooled too deeply in the military sciences to predict that any battle would be heavily one-sided, and the club-bearing army would quickly be destroyed.

Across the 30 years of my career, I have seen an ongoing change in process improvement. Some were the result of changing organizational (internal) needs and some related to customer (external) needs. Most of these evolutions arose on a seven-to-ten year cycle. They were often called "the flavor of the month" and rightly so. Despite the reputation, I looked forward to and welcomed the changes. Enter Six Sigma. Without a long dissertation, this methodology remains quite effective and utilized. As previously mentioned, I anticipated and anxiously waited for the dawn of the next evolution of process improvement and I did not see it arise.

"Analysis paralysis," "lackluster results," and on and on. These were criticisms of many projects that I led or mentored. I chalked them up to the ramblings of the uninformed. Yet over the course of more than 1,000 projects, I heard a consistent voice in a majority of them that I could not discount. "I could have saved you a lot of time, if you would have asked me in the beginning. I have been saying this for years." These comments came from the old-timers—or subject matter experts (SMEs), as we lovingly refer to them. The problem was that slightly less than half the time, they were right.

Six Sigma recognized this and reacted to this weakness by creating "parking lots" (in the event that the right answer was suggested too soon), adhering to a strict discipline (to hold off drawing conclusions), or through brainstorming and "affinitizing" (in the event that the SMEs were not as forthcoming). This bothered me. If the purpose of process improvement was to create and implement solutions, why were we so solution-averse?

I can not stand still when I see inefficiencies! At first I was called a heretic for short-cutting the Six Sigma methodology. Yet, when given a choice, the leaders of the organizations that I worked for requested me over the many disciplined practitioners. Why? My methodology produced the results that they needed, and quickly. To appease the pressure I received from my Six Sigma peers, I called the methodology DMADD (Define-Measure-Analyze-Develop-Deliver). This placated their need for discipline, while I was allowed to exercise the strengths of the new methodology.

Welcome to the 21st century! DMADD is the precision-guided missile variant of the club! Just as the club can sit next to other weapons, I do not dispute the effectiveness of the other methodologies. They still work as well as they did when they were first developed. I just do not want to fight a process improvement war with any of these methods any longer.

DMADD is the process improvement methodology of the information age. Ten to fifteen years ago, using the DMADD methodology was difficult to say the least, but enhancements to the Internet and search engines have allowed for an evolution that exceeds the effectiveness of all the previous methodologies. DMADD is solution-driven. Unlike DMAIC (Define-Measure-

Analyze-Improve-Control), it bases its effectiveness upon a base of a known or intended solution, effective solution strategies and drives to the affirmation of the original solution being correct or the implementation of a better (alternative) solution or the development of new solutions, leveraging the information derived from the analysis.

Effective DMADD process improvement requires a nimble and technically competent infrastructure. This is spelled out in detail in my forthcoming book entitled *The Perfect Machine*. But the bottom-line is still the bottom-line. The return on the investment in DMADD is huge and, most importantly, fast.

Finally, another unique characteristic is that DMADD is applicable to broad, global issues such as environmental impact. DMADD practitioners take the specialized role as an Eco-Belt and minimize the impact of an organization on the environment and directly affect the bottom line. This is spelled out in more detail in another book that I have written and will soon release, called Eco-Belt: *The Green/Greenbelt*.

Set your current club aside for a few minutes, and consider DMADD. It may be what your organization has been looking for.

Chapter 2

Organizational needs of the 21st Century

LATE in the 20th century, more often than not, the heroes in the organization were those individuals who could shoot holes in ideas and recommendations before they could be implemented. Even when these individuals were lauded for their effective use of the word "but," I warned that you became the words that you used! Overuse of that single word "but" turned a person into one (pun intended). Following the analogy of the club, these barbarians were allowed to beat potentially great ideas to death and simply walk away! Little did these organizations, who idolized this destructive skill set, realize that this behavior set put them on a course, leading to mediocrity or decline.

The organizations that quelled the "beat that thing to death" fervor, set the stage for the next generation of discovery-based, problem-solving methodologies. Enter Six Sigma. It is still a club, but one with a specific purpose. On the club's handle was an inscription that reads "For customer-focused defects only." This methodology based its success in strict adherence to a Define-Measure-Analyze-Improve-Control (DMAIC) discipline or some organizational variant. It was driven from a customer's perspective through the clear understanding of their requirements and the process' capability to meet those requirements. Making its mark initially in manufacturing settings and later in transactional and service organizations, it had its greatest success in discovering the root causes of sources of variation, first special cause (potential low-hanging fruit) and then and most significantly in the reduction of common cause (shifting the mean or average performance of a process).

In the manufacturing arena, scientific methods and many factors at a time (MFAT) pilots provided some significant results, while transactional results required a more creative skill set. As time progressed, the methodology evolved. In my opinion, it was tainted by numerous less-skilled practitioners, who succumbed to the pressure of their respective organizations, or consultants who need a fast buck and added the lean methodology to DMAIC in order to grab quick returns. I believe that DMAIC and Lean are two viable methodologies, but should *never* be melded into a single discipline. In a simple sense, Lean and Six Sigma should never be used in the same sentence without the word "and" separating them. As it currently stands, combining the two strategies is an injustice both to DMAIC and to Lean. It is more of a marketing ploy to the uninformed, and not a methodology.

We could dig deeper into the specifics of DMAIC or any of the any other methodologies. They are clubs and did (or continue to do) what they were intended to do. In most cases, they meet or had met organizational needs. Yet they did not do so without criticism. Many solutions did not last after implemented. Others took too long. Being stuck in "analysis paralysis," still others missed the mark entirely, by not gaining organizational acceptance or providing lackluster results. Astute organizations demanded a better methodology. Many killed their Six Sigma deployments. It was not because of the methodology or lack of executive support. It was the practitioners (The PI professionals, or pseudo-professionals) who are entirely to blame. These are the same practitioners who continue to write books and articles about the critical need for executive support. If these same practitioners provided organizational improvements that met the needs of the executives, they would still be employed. Until now, no one has stepped up to the plate and provided the next generation of process improvement. Enter DMADD.

There is no need to dwell on the errors of the past. A problem is still a problem, unless you bring a solution with it. Then it becomes an opportunity! Mathematically speaking:

Problem + Solution = Opportunity

Actually, "opportunity" is the difference between the performance of the current situation (problem) and the anticipated performance (solution).

Opportunity = Problem State – Solution State

No matter how we look at it, this is the crux of the 21st century solution-driven problem solving methodology!

A problem (specifically defined) with a potential solution provides us with the potential to calculate the benefit. If the benefit is large enough, we have an opportunity. From this vantage point, management can assess whether it is worth pursuing. If so, this methodology has the ability to identify one or more alternative solutions. This provides the best possible solution. This leads to an often overlooked source of impact assessment that we'll address in more detail later, called Cost of Poor Quality (CoPQ).

Briefly defined, it is the total cost of a breach of any output characteristic (Time, Volume, Quality and/or Cost; I call this TVQC) at any point within the process. More often than not, CoPQ is simply calculated as the "rework" cost associated with a defect. In order to be fully captured, rework is simply a component of a larger calculation. CoPQ is the cost associated with any deviation from perfection from the point of occurrence to the absolute end of the product's or service's life.

Organizations require quick and lasting results. More often than not, organizational impatience or subject matter expertise leads to a recommendation that is accepted without supporting data and/or validation. DMADD effectively addresses these needs.

There is a definite need for widespread application of this methodology. My greatest fear is that DMADD will be embraced by early pseudo-practitioners who claim to have "broken the code" or implemented similar methodology themselves. They may have. My warning is that, in truth, at this point, there is a very small contingent of people who have actually experienced the full extent of the methodology and can effectively execute it. Please be discerning in whom you engage.

Chapter 3

DMADD - Meeting the Needs
of the 21ˢᵗ Century Organization

"When you change the way you look at things,
the things you look at change."
—*Max Planck*

WHY is DMADD the next variation of the club? In a very elementary sense, it leverages the strengths of the current age and uses these strengths to meet the organizational needs, just as many of its predecessors did. Hidden in plain view is the first benefit. It fits!

DMADD, like the club and all subsequent weaponry, in relationship to its purpose, the concepts upon which they are based and its basic function and purpose remains the same: that is, to fix or improve existing processes.

What makes a successful process improvement methodology? The answer is easy and at the same time very controversial. PI success is the result of the creative use of the things at hand to solve the pertinent issues. I once heard it said that evolution does not produce the best possible solution, it produces a better solution. In terms of the methodology, DMADD is a step up the evolutionary ladder, carrying the DNA of its predecessors. In terms

9

of its offspring (the results of DMADD projects) it takes today's solutions and pushes them into tomorrow. This is not a claim that DMADD is the best or an "end-all" of process improvement. It is a next step. One of the "genetic improvements" that it has captured is the conscious ability to learn and adjust itself over time. This removes the curse of "static discipline" and makes it adaptive to the dynamic and fast-changing environment of this millennium.

Support and Infrastructure

As with all of the prior PI efforts, the foundation upon which DMADD is built is directly related to the organizational support structure. A building is only as strong as the foundation upon which it has been built. If there is no support, then expecting DMADD to be successful is quite unrealistic. However, if a strong foundation is established for DMADD, then the risk related to this methodology is minimized. In my upcoming book, *The Perfect Machine*, the infrastructure is thoroughly described. The level to which an organization commits to and establishes the infrastructure is directly related to the effectiveness of the methodology.

Although purely academic, DMADD has its roots firmly planted 3,000 years in the past. The Epicurean philosophy was built using a technique that chose a concept (fact) and built an entire epistemological scheme around it. The interesting point being that there was absolute consistency and coherency, and it never contradicted itself. Arguing along any point within this scheme was meaningless because care was taken to ensure that the scheme had no weaknesses.

We could learn much from this system of thought. DMADD was built using this construct. Although not yet airtight, the system is intermeshed in such a way to ensure systematic consistency. Moreover, if new discoveries arise, the system can and will be adjusted. That makes DMADD dynamic in the face of the ever-changing world in which it lives.

Every activity has been integrated into the methodology based upon the value that it can add toward the goal (to deliver a change that exceeds the required effects). Moreover, most if not all of the activities link into the DMADD methodology in multiple places so that each linkage leads to greater insight.

It should be noted that DMADD has not lost its dependence upon regression. DMADD works to "decompose" the issue and then "re-compose" a solution. Regression has proven itself time and time again as the single most effective tool in identifying change variables that truly impact the output. In a DMAIC project, the emphasis is upon building the regression equation from scratch and then verifying the impacts of the identified "x" variables and the extent to which they affect the "y." DMADD still depends upon the regression equation, but in a very roundabout fashion. It predisposes the "x" and then through hypothesis testing validates that the hypothesized "x" does in fact have the intended impact. I have termed this as "Inverse Regression."

The intent of the prior few paragraphs was to establish a flavor for DMADD and the rationale upon which it has been built. It is still in its infancy and as it is embraced by more certified practitioners it will morph, just as Six Sigma did. The worst thing that any methodology can do to itself is demand strict adherence to a structure and discipline that may not be applicable, or, worse that is outdated.

DMADD's methodological strategy is simplistically represented in the following diagram.

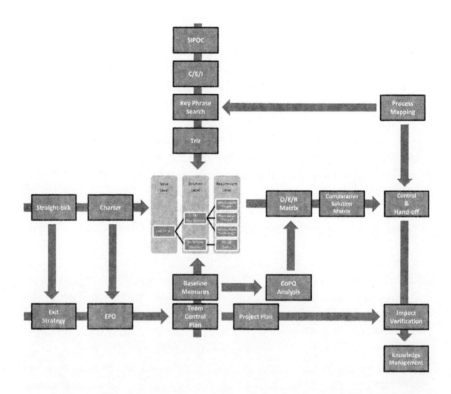

One can quickly see the DMADD methodology is not a simple linear set of activities, but linear activities nested together. This nesting allows for an extraction of as much derived value from each individual activity to the overall need of the project. All attempts have been made to minimize the activities that are simply standalone. Central to the DMADD strategy is the Solutions Tree. All activities link to (and feed) or are generated from the core activity. This leads to the final activity, which is the verification of the promised impact.

Chapter 4

DMADD – Define

"The unexamined life is not worth living"
— *The Republic; Socrates/Plato*

"The unexamined solution is not worth implementing."
— *Phil's corollary*

DELIVERABLES:

1. Straight Talk
2. Project Contract (Charter)
3. "As-Is" SIPOC
4. "As-Is" Process Map
5. VOC to CTQ to Requirements
6. Level 1 Solutions Tree
7. Level 1 Key Word Search
8. Team Control Plan
9. Baseline Data
10. Exit Strategy
11. Executive Project Overview (EPO)

PHASE GOAL(S):

- Full understanding and agreement on the issue being addressed
- Full understanding and agreement of the project expectations
- Full engagement of the team and support of the stakeholder(s)
- Full understanding of the initial recommendation
- Executive approval to pursue the project

Define

Let's begin with an explanation of the Define phase by taking us to the last question that I ask at the tollgate. After having reviewed all of the documentation, I ask:

"The project leader has a great handle on this. Would you agree with me?"

Usually this question leads to another question, but this time from the sponsor, "What do you mean by handle?"

I respond with:
- He fully understands the issue and can clearly articulate it.
- He has a thorough understanding of the process.
- He has documented the customer's and the organization's expectations of both the process and this project.
- He has clearly investigated the compliance demands and restrictions.
- He has measures in place to monitor current performance and the impact of the proposed recommendations.
- He has already begun searching out alternatives to the proposed solution(s).
- His team is assembled and everyone knows their roles and responsibilities.
- He has contingency plans.
- He has a project plan that meets the organization's need.

AND....
• He knows what it is going to take to call this project "successful and complete."

Even a tenth of a second of hesitation on the sponsor's part seems like an eternity!

When I hear an emphatic "Yes!" from the sponsor, I know that we have achieved the purpose of each of the exercises of this phase and established a foundation upon which success can be built.

The Critical Nature of Sponsorship

Before diving deeply into "Define," I feel obligated to make a brief case for project sponsorship. The factors affecting a project are numerous and vary from project to project. The bottom-line of my research into project success (spanning over 1,000 projects) is that, of all the factors, sponsor support is consistently the most critical to project success/delivery.

Of all of the define tollgates that I have been involved in, a few stand apart from the rest. The single differentiating factor was that those sponsors who walked into my office and began with that emphatic "Yes'!" not just blindly supported the effort—they knew what they were talking about. They were engaged and this project had the highest chances of success.

I dug into these specific situations because I wanted every project, to be like them. I asked; "Is the sponsor engaged because he/she is working with a great Blackbelt?" or "Is the Blackbelt great because he/she is working with a great sponsor?" The logical derivatives are countless, but you get the picture. One thing that I can say with a high degree of certainty is that when the sponsor is disengaged, the project flounders and ultimately fails no matter how competent the Blackbelt.

This discovery led to a separate sponsor certification program. It also affected our entire body of training. We now develop and teach three critical organizational components: mindset, skill set, and behavior set. I have found that when sponsors know how to think, what to use, and how to act, they are significantly more effective. This triad is in every training and development session

15

that we at The Continuous Improvement Institute (CII) now present, thanks to DMADD. I will not simply convey information and insight and then leave it in the hands of the participants to figure out how to apply it. From my experience, when you leave it in another's hands they will not apply it as you intended.

Most of the examples that I cite -- including the successful "Blackbelt" were those who, while working on projects -- kept the sponsors, (those people who are those individuals vested in the project's success, paying for it and benefiting from all of the work), abreast of every discovery and development. In most cases, the sponsor ran or participated in each individual activity. These projects performed better than any other project. The results exceeded expectations on every facet (cost, time, and impact). It was not a matter of the sponsor simply talking the talk, but walking the walk. The behavior-set is the true cost of sponsorship. This means that sponsor engagement is a necessary cost of project success. There are costs associated with any activity that involves real engagement (behaviors). We include these costs later in the calculations.

Define in DMADD is the most time-consuming and rigorous phase. The success of the effort is staged by the thoroughness and accuracy established during this step. From a DMADD perspective, process improvement success is about effecting lasting change. A building constructed on a sandy foundation will shift and settle, ending up far from what was intended by the architect; even worse, the structure will be destroyed by an onslaught of winds and storms. The same holds true for process change. Human behavior will constantly test the permanence of an implemented process change. Whether a building or a process change, if it is built upon a solid foundation, it will survive. Because clarity and agreement are important, the number of required activities within DMADD far exceed that which a traditional Six Sigma project offers, as too does the discipline and accuracy of each step. It can not be over-emphasized how critical clear definition, understanding, and agreement upon of all elements of the effort are.

In a DMAIC project, the overall focus is on the problem statement, the defect definition -- including the critical to quality (CTQ) characteristics -- the scope, and the baseline performance measure. In normal course (if one is honest with himself), insufficient time is spent on the problem statement, and CTQs. Slightly more astute practitioners pay attention to project scope, knowing that success can be defined into an effort through appropriate scoping. (If you have Blackbelts or Master Blackbelts who advocate "scope control," for that reason, stop them!) Focusing on a project's scope may predisposition the solution (in a discovery based methodology) and/or under-play or limit the effort's impact. In a worst case, the project can be misdirected entirely. (You'll find more clarification on this specific issue in the Measure phase). For the moment, avoid the creation of a project with a focus on project closure. Rather, focus development on project success and organizational impact.

The focus of a 21st century process improvement professional should be on providing the desired results--not a self-serving, "close the project" position. If they are worried about under-performing and losing their jobs, cut the chase short and end the suffering! The 21st century organization does not need under-performing, self-serving process improvement professionals and consultants draining our organizational resources under the guise of contrived success.

The focus of the Define phase in DMADD is multi-fold.
- Focus on the issue and clear definition of its impact
- Focus on the proposed solution and the real expectations
- As in project management DMADD specifically lays out the time frame expectations and the associated cost of implementation
- It also establishes "key words" that are necessary for information searches
- It also establishes the baseline from which the project springs. This includes a thorough and accurate documentation of the existing process and the measures of success (based on the customer requirements)

In DMAIC, the project begins with a "charter." In DMADD, the project starts with an exercise called "Straight Talk." Good straight talk requires much thought and effort. It is the distilled explanation of the activity. When an individual can concisely explain his or her activity, the foundation has been laid for success.

Straight-Talk

"A bad beginning makes a bad ending."
--Euripides

There are central and common tools in each PI tactic that are also used in the comprehensive PI strategy (This will be explained in the forthcoming book the *The Perfect Machine*). The beginning point in every 21st century PI effort begins with an exercise called "Straight Talk." Practitioners will see that it has sprung from the traditional and widely used "elevator speech." It was slightly changed because the elevator speech was viewed as adjunct and of little value to the overall impact to the project. That, however, was a huge mistake. Straight talk is critical and central to every PI effort. It clearly defines the project and, more importantly, sets the stage for eliciting help from the stakeholders of the effort.

A Simple Exercise that Improves Change Effectiveness

Cultural change is the penultimate exercise in rhetoric. Effective cultural change is not simply the result of a large group of people accepting the arguments of other influential people. Rather, it is the sum of the change of that population's foundational belief structure (values), operational knowledge, and habitual behaviors. It can be, and often is, argued that is culture is not changed until a majority of the population is thinking and acting differently from the previous culture.

Cultural change is an arduous task. The operating tenets of a culture are a deeply embedded, and affecting them to the point of change is often impossible. PI practitioners find a parallel situation in process change. It could be said that a process improvement (PI) initiative is simply a cultural change initiative on a significantly smaller scale. The goal of any great PI effort is to make a compelling case for change.

Although the evidence is anecdotal, many anthropologists, psychologists, and sociologists have postulated that there are few individual words that transcend cultures and ages, eliciting the same physiological reactions and responses. One word that many agree upon is the word "help!" PI professionals would be significantly more effective in their focused initiatives or their broader efforts of organizational change by effectively using this word. Given the often tenuous positions and roles of PI professionals, asking for help is extremely difficult. A challenge to make it a routine part of the "change" rigor ensued.

A simple tool has been developed to facilitate the use of the word "help." Leveraging and fine-tuning the widely used elevator speech, a tool called "Straight Talk" evolved. Since straight talk is a highly prized and valued behavioral trait, the name "Straight Talk" was tactically selected to engage both the presenter and the audience while placing a high value on the conversation.

Straight Talk is:

- A systematic effort in both creation and presentation.
- Generally developed in the initial phase of a PI effort.
- Having as many variants as there are audiences.
- Dynamic and evolving during the course of an initiative.

Like its predecessor (the elevator speech), Straight Talk is brief and to the point. It is also documented and memorized. It consists of answers to four simple but telling questions:

- What are you doing?
- Why are you doing it?
- What will it do for us?
- What do you (the audience) need to do?

Answers to the first three questions set the stage for the case for change. The final answer opens the door for a request for help. As a form, the following is an example:

Straight-Talk

1. What am I doing?	2. Why am I doing this
3. What will it do for us?	4. What do you need to do?

Form is not critical in this exercise, but content is. The more time spent developing concise answers significantly improves the effectiveness. A side benefit is that the project leader (the individual tasked with creating the straight talk) scrutinizes the real meaning of the project. In my experience, many efforts have changed as a result of this exercise.

This tool has been integrated into every aspect of the PI methodology. PI professionals are taught to create this tool and adapt it quickly to the audience at hand. Executives and project sponsors are trained to initiate these questions and expect concise answers. Moreover, this tool/exercise has application beyond project and change initiatives, in that it is being used during regular, one-on-one performance reviews, and status updates -- not to mention its use as a standard format within e-mail.

Straight Talk is a highly effective tool that sets the stage for change, whether it is at a micro-level, or the macro/organizational level. It is said that a little straight talk goes a long way. It is the natural first step leading to the more detailed charter.

20

The Project Charter

"The beginning is the most important part of the work."
--Plato

A "Historical" Case Study:
The Compelling Need for a Charter

Although this is primarily fictitious, the following story makes the case for need for a detailed charter. Let's go back in time; to a project that utterly changed the world...
The year: Sometime before 1492.
The place: The palace in Spain.
The people: Christopher Columbus and Queen Isabella.
Christopher Columbus is talking with Queen Isabella, and after making the case for an expedition across the Atlantic Ocean, with the expressed purposes of proving that the world is round.
Queen Isabella looked at this project as an opportunity to get some things that she and her country needed. She needed a fast trade route to Asia.
Queen Isabella asks, "What do you need?"
With that question, the project began.
History has been kind to this project. If it had been "chartered" and the CTQs had been documented, it would have to be reported that the purpose of the expedition was to find a better and more consistent source of opium! A few years prior, war and rebellion, drove the drug suppliers from the Iberian Peninsula. Portugal's and Spain's reliable source of that drug had been expelled from those countries and due to its addictive nature, the demand was high. Fearing a total rebellion, the "royals" set their sights on finding a cheap and consistent source.
Many possibilities were considered. The growing climate was not conducive to vertical operations. The suppliers were well known, just a bit hard to get to. The current routes were piracy-prone. The costs of obtaining the drug were way too high.
Upon hearing that the world may be spherical and that the fastest route may be in the opposite direction, the Queen jumped at the chance to sponsor it.
This is pure and entertaining conjecture, but it sets the stage

for a compelling case for chartering. The initial discussions were never documented. Yet, it seems unlikely that the sole reason for funding such a project was for purely scientific reasons. There had to be a significantly more important reason as the driving force for funding an expedition on this scale. Silk and tea are good excuses, but it had to be something much more valuable; narcotics seem to fit as an explanation.

Let's dig deeper. Fast forward a year or two!

"Land ho!" comes a cry from the crow's nest. Columbus recognizes the port. It is the one that the expedition had set out from a while back. The ships set, and immediately Columbus reports to the Queen.

She asks, "Where you successful?" and Columbus emphatically responds "Yes!"

"So you got the opium, right?" she enthusiastically inquires.

Columbus answers, "No."

"I thought you said you were successful?" she responds.

"I was," answers Columbus, "The world is round! My ships did not fall off of the edge, and I found some islands! They must be just West of India, so I claimed them for you and called them the West Indies."

"So they have opium?" she asks.

"No," he responds.

"You weren't successful, then," concludes the queen.

"How can you say that?" Columbus argues. "I proved that the world was round and found a possible route."

"You didn't get the opium," answers the queen. "I didn't want a route, I wanted the drugs. I told you not to come back unless you were successful!"

"I came back, because I was successful! I proved that the world is round and potentially found a new route!" Columbus responds defensively.

With an angry look, the queen demands "Get back out there and find those drugs! This time do not return until you find them!"

This entire discourse could have been avoided if the ancient chartering process included a review of the demands of the voice of the customer (VOC) and the voice of the business (VOB). Columbus believed that Isabella wanted one thing (which was perhaps skewed by his own agenda), and the queen wanted another (perhaps skewed by other needs). Chartering is not new or exclusive to process improvement. All major events were chartered one way or another. Most chartering occurred after the fact and was done to ensure that the efforts were adequately supplied. In this case, the project would be best served by chartering form the onset.

Every PI initiative -- in fact, every major initiative -- should be chartered. The charter is a formal contract between the project team and the sponsor and the organization. Its purpose is to clarify the problem and the expectations. It is another compelling case for the effort. Traditional charters take many different forms. Some of them are in presentation applications like Microsoft PowerPoint, others in text like MS Word; some are even available in Microsoft Excel. Independent of the format, they contain the same basic elements. These include:

- The Problem Statement – A concise description of the issue and its impact.
- The Critical to Quality expectations – The customer requirements and/or tolerances.
- The Process Scope
- The Expected Improvements
- The Team and Sponsor
- Delivery Timeframes
- The Expected Costs
- The Expected Dollar Savings

In DMADD, the initial solution to the issue is also included. At this point in the project process, this is probably the single biggest distinguishing difference between 21st century methodology and the traditional DMAIC methodology.

The following is an example of a charter commonly used in DMADD. The form layout is not critical as long as the leader, the team, the sponsor and the organization agree with all of the aforementioned aspects. Depending on the organization, signatures may or may not be necessary.

Charter

Pre-Define (to be completed by individual identifying project)

Project Specifics

Charter Approval / Results

Project Savings

As previously mentioned, it is important to document the initial recommended solution. Adjunct to that is the solution strategy. The strategy is a general description of what is being done to address the issue. It is also the first link to the "Key Phrase" search. This makes the strategy nearly as important as the solution itself. A clearer understanding of this can be seen through the use of an example.

SOLUTION

• Install a new customer dialing system.

SOLUTION STRATEGY

• Automate a manual process
• Prioritize calls based upon critical needs
• Reduce waste of time and effort

KEY PHRASES

• Effects of utilizing a dialing system to automate manual dialing
• Dialing system call prioritization
• Side benefits of utilization of a dialing system
• Innovative dialing systems
• Negative impacts of dialing systems

Although you will be reading this phrase often during this book, the importance of the charter can not be over-emphasized. It is one of those foundational activities that are important in and of itself are linked to other critical activities within the project.

SIPOC

The SIPOC is a widely recognized and often utilized tool in traditional process improvement efforts. SIPOC is an abbreviation of the major categories (supplier, inputs, process, outputs, and customers). In the vertical perspective, it is a linear breakdown of the process that is being addresses within the scope of the project. The scope should have been clearly defined in the charter. It is the beginning point of the process and the endpoint. In a general sense, the individual activities are then grouped into between five and seven process steps. Then the inputs to each step and the related suppliers are identified, as too are the outputs and the customers of each. The following document is an example of a

SIPOC utilized within the DMADD methodology:

SIPOC
☐ As is
☐ To be

Supplier(s)	Input(s)	Process	Output(s)	Customer(s)
		1		
		2		
		3		
		4		
		5		
		6		
		7	Final Product	

As a single page within the general project document, this acts as confirmation that this exercise has been completed. The details should be hyperlinked (if PowerPoint is used) cell by cell to a more detailed page or pages. I recommend that the details should include all relevant service level agreements (in the case of suppliers), performance measures (inputs), standard operating procedures (process), time, volume, quality and cost performance (outputs) and feedback (customer).

Often, the SIPOC is treated as just another "t" to cross. It is a powerful and comprehensive tool when used properly. The details that DMADD demands during the SIPOC activity forces its full potential and extracts all of the value that is hidden within it.

As it is with the charter, the "as is" SIPOC links to the key Phrase search, providing numerous possible search words and phrases. It also links specifically to the "Solutions Tree."

There are multiple SPIOCs created during a DMADD project. The "as is" is the first SIPOC developed during the project. It is the SIPOC of the existing process and acts as the baseline from which all others are compared. The "to be" SIPOC(s) are developed later (in the analyze phase), one for each alternative solution that is being entertained. Each SIPOC is compared against the baseline and against each other. When a final solution is evident, the final "to be" SIPOC is the base from which the project plan is compared in order to check and ensure that all of the critical components in the develop phase have been addressed.

This does not mean that one waits until the analyze phase to develop the "to be' SIPOCs. As information becomes available, the SIPOC work should begin. The DMADD discipline does not include absolute adherence to structure -- much to the contrary, when sufficient information is available, it is documented. Constant updating and revision assists in creating a consistent, coherent and non-contradictory project and a non-arguable solution.

"As Is" Process Map

Many define this activity as creating a drawing of the process that is involved in the project. In DMADD, it may be more appropriately called "process documentation." The purpose of process documentation is to clearly gather all of the information pertinent to the process. This could include a traditional process map, but it should also include all standard operating procedures (SOPs) and service level agreements (SLAs). Everything relevant to the process should be gathered at this step within the process. It should also be organized in a meaningful way.

The "functional" flowchart in the diagram below shows the linkage between the SIPOC and itself. Each specific SIPOC step is indicated in the chevron across the top of the form. The specific steps within the SIPOC step should be included in each vertical category and so on. I generally treat each square as an individual process map containing the steps required to add value by each contributor of the overall process. Also, if it is apparent at what step of hand-off that is causing the project's issue, it should be circled in red.

"As Is" Process Map

	SIPOC Step 1	SIPOC Step 2	SIPOC Step 3	SIPOC Step 4	SIPOC Step 5	SIPOC Step 6	SIPOC Step 7	Product
Value Add (Task hand-off)								
Value Add (Task hand-off)								
Value Add (Task hand-off)								
Value Add (Task hand-off)								

Also, this activity should also feed information and discoveries to the key phrase search. It is critical to the success of the effort to do a thorough job. The returns are directly related to the effort expended. Key words generally are in the form of verbs or what is done to the work in process.

All of this leads to one thing, and that can simply be defined as "all of the involved parties agree that the documentation is completely representative of the process."

Voices to CTQ to Requirements

In DMADD, there are six voices that potentially create tensions within a process. Those voices are:

1. The Voice of the Business (VOB)
2. The Voice of the Customer (VOC)
3. The Voice of Compliance (VOCo)
4. The Voice of the Employee (VOE)
5. The Voice of the Process (VOP)
6. The Voice of Innovation (VOI)

This activity is completed in two parts. The first activity is focused on gathering actual quotes related to each of the possible logical variants related to the six voices. This means that for each of the previously mentioned voices, there are four possible demands. They are time, volume, quality and cost. Simple multiplication shows that there are twenty-four combinations. Each of these individual components may have multiple requirements. The message is that a comprehensive capture of the voices is not a simple desktop activity.

The activity begins by capturing the "verbatim" from the relevant representatives and aligning them with the appropriate critical to quality (CTQ) characteristic. The following grid can be used to consolidate the information. No cell should be left blank. If the category is irrelevant, then that should be noted, along with proof that it is not important to the individual voice.

Philip C. Reinke

Voice Capture and Consolidation Document

Type	Source	Verbatim	CTQ (TVQC)
1T	Voice of the Business		Time
1V	Voice of the Business		Volume
1T	Voice of the Business		Quality
1V	Voice of the Business		Cost
1T	Voice of the Customer		Time
1V	Voice of the Customer		Volume
1T	Voice of the Customer		Quality
1V	Voice of the Business		Cost
1T	Voice of the Business		Time
1V	Voice of the Business		Volume
1T	Voice of the Business		Quality
1V	Voice of the Business		Cost
1T	Voice of the Business		Time
1V	Voice of the Business		Volume
1T	Voice of the Business		Quality
1V	Voice of the Business		Cost
1T	Voice of the Business		Time
1V	Voice of the Business		Volume
1T	Voice of the Business		Quality
1V	Voice of the Business		Cost
1T	Voice of the Business		Time
1V	Voice of the Business		Volume

Voice Interpretation

Running concurrently to voice capture, converting the requirements into measureable characteristics finalizes the translation. Once converted, the prioritization of the requirements is an easier task. The following table links the captured verbatim through identical columns (the first three columns). The verbatim is then interpreted from verbiage to numbers. Finally, the current process performance for each category is documented.

Type	Source	CTQ (TVOC)	Lower Tolerance	Optimum (Desired)	Upper Tolerance	Conformance (% of Output)	DPMO	Sigma
1T	Voice of the Business	Time						
1V	Voice of the Business	Volume						
1T	Voice of the Business	Quality						
1V	Voice of the Business	Cost						
2T	Voice of the Customer	Time						
2V	Voice of the Customer	Volume						
2T	Voice of the Customer	Quality						
2V	Voice of the Customer	Cost						
3T	Voice of the Compliance	Time						
3V	Voice of the Compliance	Volume						
3T	Voice of the Compliance	Quality						
3V	Voice of the Compliance	Cost						
4T	Voice of the Employee	Time						
4V	Voice of the Employee	Volume						
4T	Voice of the Employee	Quality						
4V	Voice of the Employee	Cost						
5T	Voice of the Process	Time						
5V	Voice of the Process	Volume						
5T	Voice of the Process	Quality						
5V	Voice of the Process	Cost						
6T	Voice of the Innovation	Time						
6V	Voice of the Innovation	Volume						
6T	Voice of the Innovation	Quality						
6V	Voice of the Innovation	Cost						

Completing the Activity

The activity is finalized in the following order:

- The CTQs are comprehensively captured
- The requirements of each are exactly what is demanded from each voice
- The process performance for each requirement is validated
- The characteristics being addressed within the project are identified
- The project characteristics are prioritized

Upon completion of this step, an executive update is recommended. More often than not, there are numerous discoveries that all of the stakeholders should be aware of. Discoveries often change the nature of or the expectations of the project. Clarifying the expectations of the multiple voices at the project's onset ensures a smoother journey.

Level 1 Solutions Tree

The "Solutions Tree" is the central tool of DMADD. At "Level 1" the "Solutions Tree" includes two solutions: the initial or recommended solution, and a decision to do nothing. The "do-nothing" choice establishes the baseline from which all choices are made. In some instances, the project ends with a decision to maintain the status quo and the subsequent cost of poor quality (CoPQ).

The following diagram is a basic representation of a solutions tree. In actual use, it becomes much more detailed and comprehensive.

Level 1

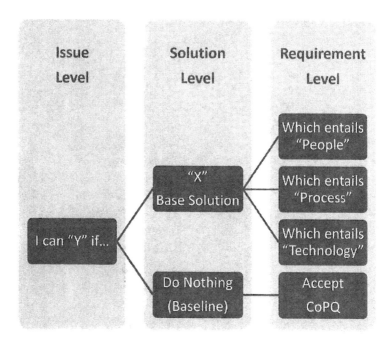

The Solutions Tree maps and documents all alternative solutions and may also feed the "Key Phrase" search. It is important to note that every alternative includes changes to people, processes and technology. The Solutions Tree documents that the project has taken all of these aspects into account. Oftentimes, ignoring one or more of these aspects, in biased favor, may provide net results that do not meet the organization's overall needs or intents.

Level 1 Key Phrase Search

"The more I learn, the more I learn the little I know."
--Socrates

The crux of 21st century process improvement and DMADD is the ability to leverage prior learning and solutions on the issue at hand. The more creative the application of information and insights gained during the search, the more impactful the effect! The "Key Phrase" search is a dynamic activity that has no limits. The only cost associated with this activity is time. The return on this investment is high. This is the hidden benefit of DMADD. That benefit is that most of the insight is gained at little or no expense, because it is from another's experience and discoveries. The Internet contains an almost endless source of information, which if leveraged properly can answer any question that an organization may have. No organization is unique if looked at from the DMADD perspective. More often than not, some other organization has encountered the issues plaguing your organization. Their solutions simply need to be ferreted out, adapted, and implemented to your benefit. One may fear that it is too large to make an impact, but that is the furthest thing from the truth.

When does the search stop? I have an axiom that I use during this activity:

"If you find yourself in a position that you have to make a decision, you do not have enough information."

Choices are not easy or profitable. I have found that risk is often the determining factor in executive decision making. If given a choice, the astute executive will choose the less risky route, which, often, sub-optimizes the effort. Directions (decisions) should be self-evident. In fact, if properly executed, there should not be a choice -- hence, no risk! DMADD seeks to make all choices no-brainers! This leads to my next axiom: "The biggest mistake that a person can make is not starting."

The key word search is another important tool of DMADD. It appears that it can be a never-ending exercise, which is not the case. The search has a definite beginning and end. Knowing where to start is not important. Simply starting is the important characteristic. That's part of the journey. The non-linear nature of a good search ensures that if it is a critical piece of information it will be captured. What is important is continuous and thorough documentation of the search. "Mind-mapping" in MS Visio is a good tool, but many other similar tools are available. Documentation and mapping the search flow is important. It precisely shows when dead ends and circles are found. The visual paths of the search are the indicators of progress and ultimately show the searcher when to stop.

If the organization has created the support infrastructure described in my forthcoming book, *The Perfect Machine*, the project leader engages the specialized expertise of the "Knowledge Manager" and mutually begins the search. The search continues until it begins to become circular in nature -- that is, no further information is gleaned from the searches or nothing new is learned. That is the endpoint. An independent set of eyes is often helpful because a project leader is under pressure to arrive at a conclusion and will often close the search too soon.

If the organization lacks a "search expert," then the responsibility falls upon team leader or one of the team members. Searching can be nearly as effective as with a "Knowledge Manager" if a few simple idiosyncrasies are addressed:

- Although they appear to be, recognize that searches are not linear in nature.

- Although one may feel tempted to do so, searches not on a single path, answers may be found in an obscure corner of the Internet!

- The initial set of key words is simply the starting point. Dynamic adjustment (the addition of new words) through discovery is critical.

- The term key words may be slightly misleading. Key phrases should be included in the search.

- It is important to document (map) every search and every path. The documentation provides the guidance and proof that the search has been completed and any additional searching will provide no additional insights.

Starting "Key Words" should be gathered from numerous sources. These include, but are not limited to:

- The Initial Solution
- The Problem Statement
- The VOC
- The CTQs
- The Requirements
- The SIPOC
- The C/E/I (Causes)
- The C/E/I (Effect)
- The C/E/I (Impacts)
- Project Goals

These categories act as a great starting point. The following template acts as the Level 1 Search. It is meant to just get the search moving and begin the discovery process.

Key Word/Phrase Search
Level 1

Reference	Key Word/Phrase	Information Captured Confirmation (+/-)	Key Learning	Abandon Or Continue

Leveraging "Triz"

In addition to describing the current state, what is trying to be accomplished should be added to the search. This is the point in which many important things can be learned and leveraged from a problem-solving methodology called "Triz." Triz has been so successfully utilized, that it is taught as a stand-alone session and it is highly recommended that any project leader be trained in this methodology. Any effective project leader should have more than a tertiary understanding of the methodology. If an organization can afford it, specific Triz expertise should be developed.

What is Triz? It is a methodology that has taken a huge amount of data related to all of the innovative solutions created in the past 100 years or so and created categories based upon the changes that resulted. Depending upon the source or Triz variant, these categories or "buckets" range from twenty to seventy. The generally accepted number of categories is forty. They are unique and exclusive to one another. Although many of them may not be directly applicable to a project's effort, the concept is applicable. A brief review of these concepts is in order. A significantly more detailed understanding of the categories and the application of each category is required to make them applicable to DMADD.

Triz Change Principles

The following list contains the forty traditional change principles. When conducting the information search, these categories can assist in expanding the search.

1. SEGMENTATION – Divide a single part or process into components.

2. TAKING OUT – Isolation of the part or component that is of value.

3. LOCAL QUALITY – Focusing quality on the individual component.

4. ASYMMETRY – Change the shape of the product.

5. MERGING – Bring similar or identical products together.

37

6. UNIVERSALITY – Make a product multi-functional.

7. NESTED DOLL – Make a product fit inside another.

8. ANTI-WEIGHT – Offset a product by lifting it with another.

9. PRELIMINARY ANTI-ACTION – Control or offset harmful effects of product's use.

10. PRELIMINARY ACTION – Perform an action before it is required.

11. BEFOREHAND CUSHIONING – Prepare reactive or emergency actions beforehand.

12. EQUIPOTENTIALITY – Limit the products potential positional changes.

13. THE OTHER WAY AROUND – Invert the actions to solve the problem.

14. CURVATURE – Use rounded surfaces rather than flat ones.

15. DYNAMICS – Design the product to optimize within the operating environment.

16. PARTIAL OR EXCESS ACTIONS – Use slightly more or less to solve issue.

17. ANOTHER DIMENSION – Change from two-dimensional to three-dimensional.

18. VIBRATION – Cause the product to vibrate.

19. PERIODIC ACTION – Change from continuous to intermittent actions.

20. CONTINUITY OF USEFUL ACTION – Make products work at full load.

21. SKIPPING – Omit steps or make process operate at high speed.

22. BLESSING IN DISGUISE – Use harmful factors to achieve positive effect.

23. FEEDBACK – Introduce feedback into the system.

24. INTERMEDIARY – Use an intermediary process.

25. SELF-SERVICE – Make a product or customer serve itself.

26. COPYING – Use a less expensive or easier copy.

27. CHEAP SHORT LIVING OBJECTS – Replace a single product with multiple products.

28. MECHANICS SUBSTITUTION – Replace a mechanical process with another method.

29. PNUEMATICS AND HYDRAULICS – Replace solid products with gas or fluids.

30. FLEXIBLE SHELLS AND THIN FILMS – Use shells and films instead of structure.

31. POROUS MATERIALS – Make a product porous.

32. CHANGE COLORS – Change the product's color or external characteristics.

33. HOMOGENEITY – Make a product uniform with its environment.

34. DISCARDING OR RECOVERING – Products that have served their purpose disappear.

35. PARAMETER CHANGES – Change the products dimensions.

36. PHASE TRANSITIONS – Use state changes to effect positive effect.

37. THERMAL EXPANSION – Use expansion to product's advantage.

38. STRONG OXIDANTS – Use oxygen-rich atmosphere.

39. INERT ATMOSPHERE – Use inert atmosphere.

40. COMPOSITE MATERIALS – Replace single materials with multiples.

There are many variations on these principles, but the basic groupings remain the same. With a creative application of the principals they can be related to any solution for any organizational issue.

Triz calls these categories principles or "change concepts." DMADD calls them "change strategies." Entertaining the "change strategy" during the "Key Phrase" search can create a very effective set of search criteria that can augment and drive the search. These will lead to many alternatives. Some time ago, a list of change concepts were shared with me. These change concepts have morphed numerous times and were adapted to "change strategies" with DMADD. If I could recall the source of the original list, I would definitely give credit where credit is due. The following "change strategies" can be leveraged into the "search" through creative thought. The easiest place to start is based in the identified changes required, found in the "Straight Talk" and "Charter" usually, in relation to the desired outcomes. The follow is the list of Triz principles converted into change concepts, converted into change strategies as adapted to DMADD:

A   Waste
B   Workflow
C   Inventory
D   Work Environment
E   Supplier
F   Customer
G   Time
H   Variation
I   System Design
J   Product/Service

Found within each of these general categories and based on the specific goals of the project, a series of expanded searches can be developed.

A. Eliminate Waste
  1. Eliminate Things That Are Not Used
  2. Eliminate Multiple Entry
  3. Reduce or Eliminate Overkill
  4. Reduce Controls on the System
  5. Recycle or Reuse
  6. Use Substitution
  7. Reduce Classifications
  8. Remove Intermediaries

    9. Match the Amount to the Need
    10. Use Sampling
    11. Change Targets or Set Points

B. Improve Work Flow
    12. Synchronize
    13. Schedule into Multiple Processes
    14. Minimize Handoffs
    15. Move Steps in the Process Close Together
    16. Find and Remove Bottlenecks
    17. Use Automation
    18. Smooth Work Flow
    19. Do Tasks in Parallel
    20. Consider People as in the Same System
    21. Use Multiple Processing Units
    22. Adjust to Peak Demand

C. Optimize Inventory
    23. Match Inventory to Predicted Demand
    24. Use Pull Systems
    25. Reduce Choice of Features
    26. Reduce Multiple Brands of Same Item

D. Change the Work Environment
    27. Give People Access to Information
    28. Use Proper Measurements
    29. Take Care of Basics
    30. Reduce Demotivating Aspects of Pay System
    31. Conduct Training
    32. Implement Cross-Training
    33. Invest More Resources in Improvement
    34. Focus on Core Processes and Purpose
    35. Share Risks
    36. Emphasize Natural and Logical Consequences
    37. Develop Alliance/Cooperative Relationships

E. Enhance the Producer/Customer Relationship
    38. Listen to Customers
    39. Coach Customers to Use Product/Service

40. Focus on the Outcome to a Customer
41. Use a Coordinator
42. Reach Agreement on Expectations
43. Outsource for "Free"
44. Optimize Level of Inspection
45. Work with Suppliers

F. Manage Time
46. Reduce Setup or Startup Time
47. Set up Timing to Use Discounts
48. Optimize Maintenance
49. Extend Specialist's Time
50. Reduce Wait Time

G. Manage Variation
51. Standardization (Create a Formal Process)
52. Stop Tampering
53. Develop Operational Definitions
54. Improve Predictions
55. Develop Contingency Plans
56. Sort Product into Grades
57. Desensitize
58. Exploit Variation

H. Design Systems to Avoid Mistakes
59. Use Reminders
60. Use Differentiation
61. Use Constraints
62. Use Affordances

I. Focus on the Product or Service
63. Mass Customize
64. Offer Product/Service Anytime
65. Offer Product/Service Anyplace
66. Emphasize Intangibles
67. Influence or Take Advantage of Fashion Trends
68. Reduce the Number of Components
69. Disguise Defects or Problems
70. Differentiate Product Using Quality Dimensions

Using the Change Strategies

Before we leave the topic of "change concepts" or "the DMADD Change Strategy," we need to understand the differences between Triz and DMADD. In Triz, the concepts are generalized and not specific enough to be applied directly to making improvements. Moreover, in Triz, the concept is considered within the context of a particular situation and then turned into an idea through creative techniques, such as brainstorming. The ideas generated lead to specific changes that can be developed, tested, and implemented in the unique and often unrelated situation. Oftentimes, what appears to be a new and unique change is often an application of one of the more general concepts, to a new situation. Solutions created through the use of Triz are still dependent upon creative talents of the team, prone to bias and still contain some risk.

In DMADD, the Triz change concepts are used as a starting point of the search. The change concepts help the team understand what changes have been effected and perfected, that will result in the required improvement. The result of the searches will provide alternative recommended changes. These turn into alternative candidates during the Develop phase within DMADD. Every alternative should be recorded and assessed for overall forecasted impact.

The relevant change concepts populate the appropriate cells within the Key Phrase Search Matrix. Over the course of a search this document can become huge! Every word and phrase utilized within the search should be captured to ensure that nothing is left unquestioned. More detail related to the change concepts will be provided later in the Measure Chapter.

Key Phrase Search Matrix

Reference	Output	Output Characteristic (TVQC)	TRIZ Concept (Level 1)	TRIZ Concept (Level 2)	Phrase Assembly	Results	New Phrase Words

Team Control Plan

"People do not fear change…they fear loss!"
"People do not oppose change…they oppose loss!"

One of the most overlooked yet important aspects related to any project are the team control plans. Although the next thought is somewhat philosophical and psychological in nature, it is worth contemplating.

All projects are about change. That old and overused axiom that defines insanity as doing the things the same way and expecting different results is subtly the reason for project failure. An improvement project may precisely identify the source of an issue or issues, it may make the perfect recommendation for change, yet the project fails because those who control the process give the change "lip service" and continue doing things the same way. The "Team Control" exercise helps to identify and address the potential roadblocks to project success.

Ultimately, it is not the team leader's responsibility to address the avoidance or opposition of individuals. If a project is sanctioned and supported by an organization, it is important that all of the relevant players work toward the same goal, whether directly involved in the project or on the periphery. It is however, the team leader's responsibility to identify concerns and address them. At that point, a discourse should ensue. If a stalemate or opposition is the result, then the roadblock is forwarded to the organization and it is addressed by the "Final Authorities."

When taken in the context of the introductory quotes, simple logic leads to:

People do not fear projects;
they fear the loss associated with the project.

People do not oppose projects;
they oppose the loss associated with the project.

It is important to understand this concept to build an effective team control plan. First it needs to be understood that the operational definition of "team" is anyone participating on the implementation of the project and/or maintaining after its implementation. The team gets very large in this context, but the success of the project depends upon all of the team supporting it and accepting the change.

The team control plan consists of a triad of tools. Included in the triad are support exercises that transition and detail communication needs. They lay out like this:

- Stakeholder Analysis
- Influence Strategy
  - Behavioral Change Strategy
  - Communication Planning Matrix
- Communication Plan

More projects have been destroyed by poor communication and lack of support (from subordinates, peers, and management). These tools, if properly utilized, minimize the chances of a lack of communication and provide a "heads-up" to management so that they can make a decision to address the personnel issue or "kill" the project.

Philip C. Reinke

The Stakeholder Analysis

A common mistake made within traditional process improvement methodologies is to define a "stakeholder" too broadly. A stakeholder is an individual who can significantly impact a project and not get fired for doing so. This makes the list of project stakeholders significantly shorter.

These are the individuals that this analysis should identify and assess. The following form is the starting point of the team control activity.

Stakeholder's Analysis

Stakeholder	Strongly Against	Against	Neutral	Supportive	Strongly Supportive	Significance
Ida Quasher	Current				Required	1
Fenz Sittor			Current	Required		5

There are four significant pieces of information on this document needed to ensure its completeness. They are:

- The specific stakeholder's name or, depending on the organization, a code that identifies the individual anonymously.
- Current Support Posture. This should be hyper-linked to a separate document that spells out (in detail) the specific concerns, etc.
- Required Support Posture. As with the previous "posture" this field should be hyper-linked to a detail page with the rationale behind the required assessment.
- Significance to the project's success. This too is hyper-linked to a rationale page.

A good general rule of thumb is that this activity is not openly shared. I have seen some projects and careers nearly destroyed by broad distribution of this information. This is probably the single document that is shared on a need-to-know basis only.

Behavioral Change Strategy

This exercise focuses on the behaviors elicited by the stakeholder. The verbal support given by a stakeholder is a nice starting point, but what they do is significantly more important (and measureable). All ends of the behavioral spectrum should be addressed. This exercise should identify what behaviors need to be created and which should be suppressed. There are four elements important to this activity. They are:

- The specific stakeholder's name. As before, this may be coded.

- The required behavior. This should be a list of those required to be more prevalent and those that should disappear.

- Success status. This is constantly updated with the most relevant observations.

- Discoveries and actions. This in combination with "status" makes the document dynamic and living. During the course of addressing the behaviors, discoveries may change the plans and activities.

Behavior Change Strategy

Stakeholder	Required Behavior (More/Less)	Success Status	Discoveries & Actions

Once the stakeholder's issues and behaviors are being addressed, it is important not to lose sight of organization on the whole. That is the purpose of the next two activities.

The Communication Planning Matrix

Broad communication of a project or initiative helps drive success from two directions. First, it is a visible commitment of the team to the effort. The effort is in the spotlight, and the team members are more motivated not to fail in front of the entire organization. Second, it acts as a channel for eliciting assistance and communicating organizational expectations.

The following matrix is pre-populated with most of the common and effective media channels (in the "method" column). It is not an all-inclusive list; media can be added and deleted as best fits the organization.

During the course of the project, beyond the executive project update, there are significant communication events. They are:

- Project announcement or "kickoff." Everyone should be aware of the effort.

- Project objectives. Although these are communicated at kickoff, continuous clarification is critical.

- Organizational unification. This is continuous communication of the value propositions of the project. It is communicating the compelling case for change.

- Status. Keeping the project's status in the forefront of the organization's mind—and that it is making progress—is important.

- The official implementation announcement is as important as the project kickoff. This is when the organization realizes that it is a "new age." These announcements can also quell insecurities through training announcements and the like.

Communication Planning Matrix

Method (Media)	Project Kick-off	Sharing and Clarifying Objectives	Organizational Unification	Status Updates	Change & Training
Publications: • Email • Postings • Newsletter • Website					
Mass Communication: • All Employees • Staff Announcements • Focused Meetings • VM Announcements • Podcasts					
Individual Communications: • Straight-Talk • EPO (Stakeholders) • Project Team					
External Communications: • Customer • Conferences • Media					

Because the individual cells are small, it is recommended that the hyper-link to more detailed documents be utilized. This document should link to the communication plan and the overall project.

The Communication Plan

The final activity within the team control plan is the communication plan. Utilizing the information provided by the assessments and creating realistic stakeholder expectations, along with the organizational communication needs, a comprehensive plan should be created. This plan should take care of every detail to ensure that the plan is implemented as expected.

The details of this plan should feed the overall project plan, which is finalized in the develop phase. The team leader should use this as a control document and be responsible for its ongoing update and revision.

49

Communication Plan

Audience	Objective	Message	Method (Media)	Who	Timing & Location

Baseline Data (Output Measures)

There are no standard forms for representing the baselines (output measures) in DMADD. Yet, there are two important characteristics of this activity. Both characteristics directly relate to representation. First, that the baseline measures are actually representative of the process' performance; second that the sponsor and stakeholders agree that the measures are representative of the process and will be affected by the recommended solution.

Baseline measure should be focused on the final output of product. There should be at least four specific measures. They are:

- *Time.* The total processing time from order or process trigger to the customer's acceptance of the product (processing time per unit).

- *Volume.* The output count, or the number of products produced during a specific and significant timeframe (e.g. units per day).

- *Quality.* Multiple measures can exist here. They can include the percentage of time that the production meets customer requirements or the percentage of failures. It could be counts of successes or failures or a measure of a specific defect type. All of the voices should be measured.

- *Cost.* The processing cost per unit.

Development of the baselines or utilization of existing measures is not a one-time event. It is the starting point from which continuous monitoring of the process is established and distributed to the sponsor and stakeholders. These may change upon discovery, but once established they must be maintained in order to show the impact of any the final changes and that the project requirements have been met.

Exit Strategy

"Success is a matter of luck, the harder one works,
the luckier they get."
--Gary Player

A New Tool to Mitigate the Effects
of "Scope Creep" and Ensure Project Closure

During the define stage of the traditional DMAIC methodology, a charter is prepared with the express purpose of problem clarification, specifying customer requirements, developing baseline performance, and establishing improvement goals. Despite gallant efforts, a DMAIC project often falls prey to what DMAIC practitioners call "scope creep."

Although scope creep has many root causes, adding a simple exercise/document in the initial project stage helps to ensure project focus and sets the stage for smoother project closure. This tool is called the exit strategy.

As the name implies, the exit strategy defines what it takes to close the effort. It is tactically placed as a separate step within "define" and is the final deliverable of this phase for many reasons. First, its purpose is to clearly define project expectations. Second, it requires formal agreement with those definitions of success. Lastly, it is positioned as the final deliverable in the stage, to emphasize the fact that the project has a specific beginning and end.

Simplicity is at the core of this exercise and little or no explanation is required to effectively utilize it.

Philip C. Reinke

Exit Strategy

This effort is specifically focused on:
1. (Time)
2. (Volume)
3. (Quality)
4. (Cost)

This effort will be considered complete when:

What?	How Much?
1. (Time)	
2. (Volume)	
3. (Quality)	
4. (Cost)	

Sponsor: _____ Date: _____

PI Leader: _____ Date: _____

The form is not critical; however, the contents of the example have been refined over 100 projects. These components can be placed into four specific categories. They are:

- *Measureable characteristics.* These are the specific process output CTQs that are to be addressed by the project. The project may address one or more of these CTQs, either the amount of processing time, output volume, product quality, or product/processing cost.
- *Specific project-deliverable expectations.* This takes measurable characteristics one step further and defines "what" the expected deliverables are.
- *Quantity and frequency of the deliverables.* This ensures that "how much" and "how often" is also clearly defined.

- *Signatures of agreement.* By reviewing this document and formally agreeing upon the expectations the project sponsor and Process Improvement Leader can revisit this document on any occurrence of project slippage or scope creep.

Projects often convert from a short-term effort focused on a specific issue to a long-term career because of "scope creep." Through clear definition of "what" and "how much" is expected, along with participant agreement will significantly aid in ensuring project success.

The 5ᵗʰ Element (Measureable characteristic) of a DMADD Project

I previously mentioned that I have challenged myself and others to identify the measureable elements of a process' output beyond TVQC (time, volume, quality and cost). No one has risen to the occasion. Yet there is a fifth performance measure that is of significance to an organization that, more often than not, is the true driver of organizational decisions. The interesting thing about this fifth element is that there are often no numbers attached to it even though there should be. That element is called the cost of poor quality (CoPQ). This term has been tossed around for some time and I do not know its exact origin. The problem that I have seen in its use is that those who refer to it do not fully understand its real definition. As a result, it is obscure and theoretical rather than precise and powerful.

Gaining a real understanding or definition of CoPQ is much like a scoping exercise. We could use tools like "In-the-Frame/ Out-of-Frame" to draw a picture of it. Rather, let's just make two lists. I call this exercise "What it is/What it isn't."

What it isn't:

- The cost of production, specifically within the process (operating costs)
- Reworking costs internal to the process (as long as the unit leaves the specific process meeting customer's requirements)

- Reworking costs associated to "fixing" an input to the process (this is someone else's CoPQ)

What it is:

- Any rework or preparation cost assumed by the recipient or a customer of the process, when it is associated with an error or breach in the output requirements.
- Lost revenue due to a client's need for higher quality or bad press
- Customer service-related costs (warranty, complaint costs, litigation)

A good general rule of thumb is that the CoPQ is all the downstream costs associated with the process' output that does not meet a direct or indirect customer's requirements within the categories TQVC.

The following diagram is used to represent the full gambit of measures related to a project, and will make its appearance throughout the project to ensure that the measures stay in the forefront of the stakeholder's minds.

Allow me to take the literary license to anthropomorphize CoPQ: It is a hidden beast that devours margins as if it were the dessert of its existence. Many organizations refuse to recognize the true impact of the CoPQ. When margins hover in percentages in the twenties or lower, there are generally efforts made to bolster them. Many organizations take the route of attempting to improve efficiencies, cutting positions and associated operational costs. This is the beginning of an organization's demise, which starts the vicious circle and spirals it to a point of no return.

I have worked in many organizations in which the sales force's size was continuously increased with the excuses that the market has become more competitive, or the clients are of poorer quality, or that the sales leads quality has declined...and so on...

More often than not, and with deeper analysis, the decline coincides with an aggressive growth plan, breakdowns in the terms of engagement used by the sales force, increases in sales quotas/goals, and downstream processes that are not robust enough to handle the changes in the general nature and composition of the broader clientele.

The leaders of the "engagement" groups sit at the front end of the process and declare incorrectly that the rest of the organization is incompetent and error-ridden. This leads to ruination. The fact of the matter is that it is the sales group who is supplying poor quality input—and their CoPQ is huge!

Organizations would be much better served by maintaining or reducing the size of the sales force, and ensuring that the CoPQ from them is minimized downstream. As a general rule of thumb, if an organization has a margin at, for example, 20 percent, a good portion of the operating costs are consumed by CoPQ. Striving for complete upstream minimization of CoPQ can change the course of the organization and its subsequent health. DMADD is perfectly suited to addressing these types of issues.

Enough has been said about CoPQ. It is a fundamental, complex, and critical element that organizations need to fully grasp in order to ensure their long-term viability. An entire book can be dedicated to this concept (and probably will). Any organization that strives for 21st century survival needs to focus resources on the CoPQ and take control of it. The result of not doing this will have terrible consequences.

The Executive Project Overview (EPO)

The rationale for driving into a rather long discussion about the CoPQ is that it is a critical part of the executive project overview (EPO). In the early stages of a project it is important to work with the stakeholders and sponsors, gaining agreement on what their needs are relative to status updates and requests for assistance. This sets the stage for clear and effective communication. The EPO is a dynamic tool that ensures that the decision-makers are kept abreast of the project's developments and discoveries. It also acts as the trigger to project supportive behaviors from the decision-makers. When this is utilized in combination with an updated straight talk, the project timeline should almost automatically stay on track—that is, if the sponsor and other relevant stakeholders respond appropriately and timely.

The EPO includes information that, at a glance, reminds the sponsor and stakeholders of:

- The project name and purpose
- The Project timeline
- The expected impact areas (TVQC & CoPQ)
- What has changed since the last update
- What assistance is required to keep the project on track

The EPO also gives the project sponsor and/or stakeholders the option to cancel the project at any juncture or discovery. Finally, the EPO indicates through actual or auto-signature that the sponsor and/or stakeholders have reviewed the project and are aware of the status and its demands for continuation. This is important to ensure that all relevant parties are never blind-sided of information.

An unspoken role of the EPO is to guide the sponsors and/or stakeholders along the path of discovery. Since its conception, in more than 80 percent of the cases, the initial solution documented was not the solution that was implemented. At first this was an alarming discovery. Over time, it became understood, yet the projects were slowed while the decision-makers were brought up to speed around the rationale for the changes in the solutions.

The EPO makes updates and discoveries a matter of due process, and delays in the project have been minimized.

An example of the EPO document follows. It can be varied according to organizational and individual needs.

Some effective tactics are included in its preparation. All new information or changes must be in a unique font color. We use red. Any changes are hyper-linked to supporting documentation, providing sufficient detail to make the overview understood. If additional information is required, the overview is not signed or initialed, until all parties agree.

With agreement on the layout, content, and frequency of updates for the EPO, the project is now staged to move into its next DMADD stage (Measure). For the traditional DMAIC practitioner, the next stage may be a bit confusing. I simply ask that you allow story to progress, and it will make sense in the end.

Chapter 5

DMADD – Measure

DELIVERABLES:

1. Data Collection Plan and Verification
2. Process Baseline Validation
3. C/E/I Diagram
4. Level 1 Opportunity/Effort/Risk Matrix
5. Expanded Key Phrase Search
6. Process/Project Model
7. Executive Project Overview Update (EPO)

PHASE GOALS:

- Create and verify the data that supports the baseline measures and all subsequent data that will be used throughout the project
- Create and verify the cause and impact of the issue to be addressed by the project
- Create and validate the real cost of the recommended solution
- Development of a base process model to use in the as-

sessment of the recommended solution and all subsequent solutions

- Executive support to develop solutions

By this point in the DMADD project I often hear, "Get on with it!" A lot of time is spent in the defining stage of DMADD and from this point on, the rate of project increases significantly. There are fewer deliverables and a majority of the work is focused on solution verification, selection of the best fit and implementation (as you'll see in subsequent chapters).

The Measure phase in the traditional DMAIC methodology focuses on gathering data and background information that will be utilized in the Analyze Phase. It has a specific beginning and end. The measure phase in DMADD is the same in relation to the gathering of data-related to the base, except that it is related to the initial solution. It is different in that it is iterative, and repeats itself with the discovery of each and every viable solution. It sets up a data set and a process model to test each according to the changes in the process. At this juncture in the methodology, the emphasis is on the establishment of baseline measures upon the effectiveness of each and final solution will be judged.

The primary tools driving this phase are the "Level 1 Solutions Tree" and a model. The "Level 1 Solutions Tree" was developed in the prior phase and may (and perhaps should) be modified with each discovery. One will notice that one of the alternatives on the tree is to do nothing. This alterative is the current data set. If or when the base data set are altered or modified, this alternative should be altered, too. Therefore, all of the baseline metrics are aligned with this option. From this point only can the effectiveness of all alternative solutions be ascertained.

The process model should be developed to suit the project. It may be as simple as segmenting the data in a way to show the impact of each solution, or it may be a complex software system. The decision on which modeling methodology to use is strictly a decision of the organization and its confidence on its representation of the proposed change's impact. A word of caution to practitioners: Be careful not to get caught up in the process model. Its purpose is simply to model the intended impacts of the proposed changes. Many practitioners get caught up in the beauty of a model and waste precious time.

The best way to develop a "workable" model is to develop it in reverse and test it against the most elementary alternatives. Whatever model is chosen, the important aspect is that agreement of its representation is needed to ensure that the model is representative of the process and the expected impacts of the process changes are also representative. Before this can happen, it is necessary to gather and address any arguments against the model's results. This takes place in two parts. It is first accomplished through a confirmed data collection. When the data that is to be used within the model is agreed upon, the biggest hurdle is jumped.

Data Collection Plan

In traditional DMAIC, most of the activity in the measure phase is focused on finding and validating data and basic process information. As a result, Gage R&R and Measurement Systems Analyses occupy a great amount of this phase's activities. This is somewhat true in DMADD. Our methodology continues refining the activities of gathering and verifying, the process and performance information which began in the define phase. More important at this point, the activity is focused on agreement. Whether the information is in the form of a data set, or a graph or a report or a process map, the stakeholders need to verify that they agree that the information is truly representative of the process. Once the data set or data source is confirmed the model can be tested with it to ensure that the model replicates reality.

DMADD Consolidated Data Sources

Data Description	Purpose or Intended Use	Data Source Verified by:	Stakeholder Confirmation (Representation)
1. (Time)			
2. (Volume)			
3. (Quality)			
4. (Cost)			

This form does not look much like a traditional DMAIC "Data Collection Plan." That traditional form may be used to augment the consolidated data sources sheet. This form is at the top level of activities and, as with previous DMADD forms, is the confirmation of the activity completion. Significantly more detail is required to ensure that the data is relevant. In almost every case the individual cells within this form are hyper-linked to more detailed information. Examples of the linkages include:

- *Data description.* A link to an actual data sheet, a more detailed data collections plan, Gage R&R, MSA, charts, graphs or reports.
- *Purpose or intended use.* A link to a detailed page that explains the data's current utilization and what purpose it will serve in the project.
- *Data Source Verification.* Generally the only cell not linked.
- *Stakeholder confirmation.* Although this captures the comprehensive list of stakeholder's confirmations, it may be linked to a document that has their reservations or concerns. This activity would feed prior influence strategies (in reverse) and the project plan in future phases.

I can not over-emphasize that the most important piece of this activity is the stakeholder's confirmation. Attempting to railroad results, impacts, or the project in general, by shortcutting this step will only result in rework later in the project of less than anticipated results. On the opposite side of this equation, a stakeholder who agrees with the data's integrity and representation will find it difficult to disagree with the analysis and recommendations if they are based upon their own data. The icing on the cake— and a final and important step which should be included in this activity— is the formal verification that the baseline data and graphs are representative of the process' performance. This should be the last entry on the sheet.

Moving from the confirmation of the data and its representation of the process' performance, it is time to move to the identification of the potential sources or causes of the issue. This will be accomplished through the use of the following activity.

Cause/Effect/Impact

The traditional Ishikawa diagram (commonly referred to as the "fishbone" diagram) is the starting point from which the assessments of the development of effective solutions are built. In DMADD, the cause/effect diagram has been enhanced to include the related impacts of each of the effects. This converts the well-known C&E diagram into a DMADD C/E/I analysis.

In DMADD, as with traditional process improvement efforts that use the C&E diagram, the best use of this diagram is to include a "data-driven" validation of the hypothesized causes. Although statistical validation is preferred, simple segmentation may be sufficient to validate the causal connection. Keep in mind that the better the correlation between the effect and the cause, the better the model will function.

After the C/E portion of the activity is completed, a systematic effort is required to ascertain the impact of each of the driving (significant) causes. This information and insight feeds subsequent assessments, later in the project.

Also, another series of key phrases can be (and this is often the case) gathered from the C/E/I diagrams, and fed to the "Key Phrase" search. The search strategies may change significantly as a result of discoveries in this activity. It is important to pay special attention to categorical searches which fall into three categories: causes, effects, and impacts. We'll dive deeper into this discussion later in this chapter.

Cause/Effect/Impact Diagram

Taking the Ishikawa Exercise One Step Further to Enhance Project Performance

In the 1960's Kauro Ishikawa developed the cause/effect (C&E) analysis for the Kawasaki organization. It was quickly accepted by the process improvement (PI) community. The C&E's systematic simplicity and effectiveness have made it a widely used and, often, an essential deliverable in traditional quality efforts.

Over the course of 40 years, the use of the C&E as a single quality improvement tool has seemed to wane, but the effectiveness of it as a tool (when used properly) has not. The C&E exercise appears simple, yet it requires thorough and data supported effort to maximize its effectiveness. Many process improvement practitioners lost the connection between the C&E diagram and the mathematical relationship it has to a project. This loss of connections has resulted in this exercise becoming another check mark type effort.

Because of the consulting nature of process improvement and the emphasis on "speed of project delivery," the C&E is often given tertiary emphasis; it was treated like the aforementioned diagram and it therefore lost its value. Moreover, many organizations easily recognize the cause-effect linkage, but fail to link the effects to organizational impact. Originally it was assumed that the users were also keenly aware of the impact. I am finding that organizations need to see the impacts on paper as much as they

64

need to see the C/E relationship.

The C&E analysis, as a tool, can be return to its original powerful impact through proper timing of the analysis and completing it, in the way it was originally intended. Doing so will allow it to extract the full value of this exercise.

Why Times Five

Before we go too deep into the C&E and subsequently into the Impact, "I," we need to preface with a discussion of root cause analysis. As previously noted, the C&E is an anecdotal tool that directs the user towards potential root causes of an issue. The work with the C&E is often too superficial to be effective.

This weakness can by overcome through strict adherence to a discipline of asking "Why?" five times, for each individual causal path, that is being investigated. Most practitioners avoid this activity, because it brings to mind the annoying behavior of a three-year-old." Let's look into this activity a bit deeper.

On their way to adulthood, children go through many stages. At the age of three, they focus on "information acquisition" or become learning machines (this does not assume that they were not prior to this age). Their focus is on acquiring as much learning as possible. Temporal permanence has disappeared, and they are growing in their awareness of the world around them.

Over the course of human evolution, humans have developed basic instincts that promote efficiency. Information acquisition is a prime example. I have personally tried this and also challenge DMADD candidates (who have three-year-olds around them) to do the same. When a child asks "Why?" answer him and wait. He will ask again, and you answer him accordingly. He will repeat "Why?" four or five times and then quit.

I used to chalk this up to attention span, but I soon saw that this behavior was ingrained in most every child that I did this with. "Why?"

Over time, humans have evolved and unconsciously learned that after asking "Why?" four or five times, they have arrived at the real answer for their initial question—or annoyed the respondent so much that their safety was compromised, Seriously, there is little or no benefit in asking seven or more times. Children innately hold a key to efficient and effective information acquisition, and we avoid it. "Why?" times five is in our DNA because it works!

Another interesting observation is that, over the course of thoroughly documenting hundreds of processes, when properly developed, they decompose into about five levels of detail. At the fifth level, documentation usually consists of individual steps. If an issue exists at the highest level, as one drives deeper into the related processes, the track that the inquisition takes ends at a task or a step, at level five.

This means that asking "Why?" fives times will take one to the point where the error is really created—the root cause. Given these two bits of trivia and my experience with success, in adherence to this technique, I am a strong proponent of "Why times five."

Given these assumptions, let's go back to the diagram and drive to a root cause.

W1– Why is this issue occurring? Answer: MANAGE-MENT (W2)

W2– Why is Management the cause of this issue? Answer: W3

W3– Why is W3 creating this? Answer: W4

W4– Why does this specifically affect the result? Answer: W5!

Is it annoying? Yes.

Is it effective? Yes, emphatically!

As with other exercises within the project documentation, the single page acts as confirmation that the exercise was adequately conducted. Details should be hyperlinked (if using PowerPoint) to additional pages.

Also, every logical path across each of the "6 Ms" should be followed and confirmed, so as to leave no stone unturned. As much value is derived, from "dispelling myths" and verifying "what it is not" as there is in identifying "what it is!"

Impact – The Missing Element

I have found that many of the students of the late 20th century, who are now adults in the 21st century are astute at identifying the cause/effect relationship, but terrible at drawing the linkage to the true impact of the effects. As a result, I have expanded the cause and effect diagram (C&E) to the cause-effect-impact diagram (C/E/I).

As I previously stated, for more than 25 years, I have challenged practitioners to identify any critical, output characteristics beyond the categories of time, volume, quality, and cost. No one has been able to! As a result, I suggest that for each effect, each logical path (the 6Ms) is followed and each output characteristic is entertained. As is true in the reverse analysis, used to ascertain the root cause, the same holds true from the effect through the impact—that is, knowing there is impact is as important as identifying that there is no impact.

The C/E/I plays a critical role in expanding the number of possible solutions in addition to assessing the real impact of the initial solution on the expected outcome. It helps remove the associated risk and drives the project towards making acceptance of the solution a no-brainer.

Level 1 - *Opportunity/Effort/Risk*

I remember when I first learned about the opportunity/effort analysis. I grabbed it and over-used it. The matrix that was presented looked much like this:

Opportunity/Effort Grid

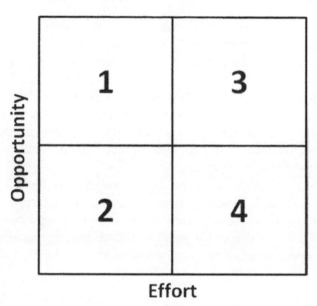

The exercise was very easy, and put efforts into a good perspective. Let's refresh our memories on how it is used:

- The opportunity axis – as one moves vertically, upward, the opportunity afforded by the change is greater

- The effort axis – as one move horizontally from left to right, the amount of effort required to implement the change grows

- The best options are those falling in the "1" quadrant (highest opportunity, lowest effort)

- The worst options are those falling in the "4" quadrant (lowest opportunity, greatest effort)

For theoretical explanation of the prioritization concept, this grid was perfect, but I (and many others) took it literally and attempted to put values around both the opportunity scale and the effort scale. Although I made it work, many times it failed to give me a true customer/organization serving priority.

When I stepped back and reviewed the successes and failures, I found that I was applying an open-to-argument," two-dimensional activity to a three-dimensional world! I then set about searching for that missing element, in hope that discovering it would take this already brilliant activity and make it truly applicable to the efforts of our project work. In short order I found that the element was risk. In a pictorial/theoretical sense, the new matrix looks something like this:

Opportunity

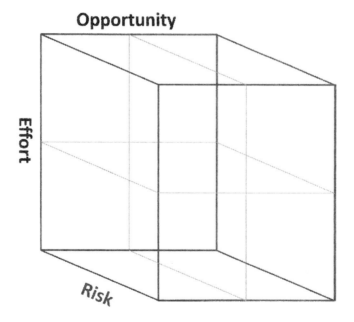

The opportunity/effort elements of an effort remain exactly the same, but the element of risk puts decisions on a parallel track with what really occurs in organizations. Risk is defined as the probability of the effort occurring as it is intended. Going back to one of my guiding axioms: "If you find yourself in a position that you have to make a decision, you do not have enough information."

We find that risk can be minimized through the extensive capture and translation of information. Therefore, risk is actually an assessment of not what we know, but what we do not know. This is difficult, but achievable. In this diagram, risk grows as one moves front to back. That means that that less information that one has, the more risk that the organization must assume.

Putting this into a workable tool is not difficult. A simple Excel grid is often utilized. The following is an example:

O/E/R Matrix

Solution	Opportunity	Effort	Risk	(O x E x R)

On the O/E/R matrix each element can be given a numeric value. A good starting point is simply comparing the total list of solutions to each other and giving them a high, medium, or low ranking for each respective category. Then assign a numeric rating of 1, 2 or 3 to each. Beginners often make the mistake of incorrect assignments. They are as follows:

- Opportunity – Low = 1, Medium = 2, High = 3
- Effort – Low = 3, Medium = 2, High = 1
- Risk – Low = 3, Medium = 2, High = 1

Next, the individual rankings are multiplied in the rightmost column and sorted in descending order. Oftentimes, more resolution is required. Providing it is simply a matter of building a more comprehensive operational definition of each category.

This activity sets the initial stage for ongoing prioritization of solutions and points to where more information is required (high risk). An important aspect of the activity is the documentation of the reasons for eliminating one of the options. The reason for an option not carrying forward to the next prioritization iteration needs to be as fully explained as the rationale for those that do. The O/E/R activity also indirectly narrows search criteria. I have, however, found that other key words or phrases arise as the effort prioritizes the solutions. Careful attention should be paid to these when they arise.

Key Word Searches

Mentioned earlier in the chapter was the use of the C/E/I in expanding the "Key Word Search." As is true with the O/E/R activity, and as the C/E/I is developed, the practitioner must be keenly sensitive to the recurring words and phrases that pop up is investigating the logical paths. An interesting observation is that these phrases often parallel the traditional Triz or change concepts activity and can be categorized the same as in those used by it. As previously noted, there are many variations of the Triz and the change concepts categories. Although noted earlier, I have expanded on the definitions of the each, so as to perhaps generate additional thoughts around searches. The general categories and the details behind each that have been found to be the most applicable to DMADD are as follows:

Eliminate Waste

In the broadest sense of the term, any input (activity or resource) in an organization or a process that does not add value to an external customer can be considered waste. Solutions based on waste reduction more often than not provide significant returns on investment.

1. *Eliminate things that are not used.* Constant change in organizations or processes results in a change in demand for specific resources and activities (inputs). At one time these inputs were important to the business, product, or service, but changes in customer demands changed those components. Constant reassessment is required. Numerous solutions to this type of waste have been implemented with great results. Unnecessary activities

and unused resources can be identified through various activities such as surveys, audits, data collection, and analysis of records. It is critical to ensure that the unused element (waste) which was removed from the system does not return.

2. *Eliminate multiple entries.* In some situations, information is recorded in logs or entered into a database, more than one time, creating no added value. This situation is called data redundancy. Technological solutions to this issue is easy to find and quick to implement. Changing the process to require only one entry can lead to improvement in productivity and quality by reducing discrepancies or entry errors.

3. *Reduce or eliminate overkill.* As a natural result of risk aversion, a company's standard or recommended resources are designed to handle special, severe, or critical situations rather than the normal situation. Changing the standard allocations, to the appropriate level of resources for the normal situation will reduce waste. Additional resources would be used only when warranted. Many different strategies have effectively addressed overkill.

4. *Reduce controls on the system.* Individuals and organizations utilize various types of controls to make sure a process or system does not stray too far from standards, requirements, or accepted practices. While useful for protection of the organization, these controls can increase costs, reduce productivity, and stifle improvement. Traditional controls include a layered management structure, approval signatures, standardized forms, and reports. Regular reviews of all of the organization's control procedures, by everyone working in the system, can result in identifying opportunities to reduce controls on the system without putting the organization at risk. Aligning the organization with the latest developments in control has long-term benefits.

5. *Recycle or reuse.* Once a product is created and used, it is natural to discard it and the by-products created by its use. However, if other uses can be found for the discarded product or by-products, the cost of production can be spread out over its use and its reuse. The green movement has brought to light many creative solutions that can lead to additional revenue to engaged organizations. (This topic had been addressed in significantly more detail in my forthcoming book, *Eco-Belt: The "Green" Greenbelt.*)

6. *Substitute.* There are many examples of substitution. One includes the elimination of waste. It can often be reduced or eliminated by replacing some aspect of the product or process alternatives. Value engineering is one type of substitute to include lower-cost components, materials, or methods that do not affect the performance of the process, service, or product. But substitution should not be limited to product components they can include switching to another process having fewer steps or more automation. The substitution strategy is often utilized at a high-level and should be considered also at a granular level.

7. *Reduce classifications.* Classifications are often developed to differentiate elements of a system or to group items with common characteristics, but these classifications can lead to system complexity that increases costs or decreases quality. Classification should be reduced when the complexity caused by the classification is worse than the benefit gained. Reclassification is a solution that can often be implemented without a significant cost.

8. *Remove intermediaries.* Organizations often use intermediaries such as distributors, handlers, agents, and carriers as part of a system. This was often done to reduce cost without full consideration of the CoPQ. Some intermediaries add value to a process because of their specialized skills and knowledge, but this should be con-

tinuously assessed. This solution can be a double-edged sword. Benefits can be derived in a short term with long term consequences.

9. *Match the amount to the need.* Oftentimes organizations create standard sizes or quantities without regard to real customer needs. Organizations can often adjust products and services to match the Customer need. Doing so reduces waste and excess inventories. This solution often engages parts of the organization that traditionally is not part of PI (marketing and sales).

10. *Sampling.* Organizations use reviews, checks, and measurements for a variety of reasons. Often, the entire population is monitored and measured to ensure accuracy, to avert risk. Answering a simple question—can these be measured without checking or testing everything—often pays high dividends. Solutions often include cutting edge analytic methods and technology/automation.

11. *Change targets or set points.* Organizations often establish targets and set points for various reasons and these targets create ongoing issues. Reassessing the rationale behind their establishment is important. Research may include the customer requirements and alternative equipment to providing specific product/service obligations at cost-effective levels.

Improve Work Flow

Products and services are delivered to customers through processes. Changes in process workflow are often the solution to organizational performance issues.

12. *Synchronize.* The production and delivery of products and services usually involves multiple stages. These stages operate at different times and at different speeds, resulting in an operation that is not smooth. Synchronization has been used effectively in such situations.

13. *Schedule into multiple processes.* Linear thinking often creates a one product/one process system. A robust system can be designed capable of producing multiple versions of the product from a single process that is focused on the specific requirements of the service/product. Rather than a "one-size-fits-all" large process, multiple versions of the process are available, each tuned to the different types of needs of customers or users. Priorities can be established to allocate and schedule the inputs in order to maximize the performance of the system. The solution has been effectively utilized within the automotive industry with many cross-applications

14. *Minimize handoffs.* More often the case, systems require multiple handoffs. Components such as data, forms, or the product itself are often transferred to many people, offices, or work stations to complete the processing or service. The handoff from one stage to the next can increase time and costs and increase the risk of quality problems. The work flow can be rearranged to minimize any handoff in the process. This solution is prevalent within automation schemes and is effective in routine situations.

15. *Move steps in the process close together.* Organizations that jumped on the off-shoring bandwagon are often plagued with this issue. The physical location of people and facilities can affect processing time and quality. Physically finding locations of sequential process steps adjacent to each other can be effective in eliminating issues. This eliminates the need for communication systems, such as mail, and physical transports, such as vehicles, pipelines, and conveyor belts and the associated costs. Do not limit this series of solutions to the physical realm. Virtual relocation oftentimes is effective also.

16. *Find and remove bottlenecks.* This solution was very popular a decade ago and still applicable today. A bottle-

75

neck is any situation in which the production capacity is exceeded by the input capacity. A constraint within an organization would be any resource for which the demand is greater than its available capacity. To increase the throughput of a system, these must be identified, exploited if possible, and removed if necessary. Bottlenecks occur in many parts of daily life; they can usually be identified by looking at where people are waiting or where work is piling up. Many are hidden through poor service level agreements (SLAs). Many innovative bottleneck and constraint reduction solutions exist. Their creative application can impact an organization almost immediately.

17. *Use automation.* Any repetitive task can and should be automated. The flow and capacity of many processes can be improved by the intelligent use of automation. Consider the automation solutions to improve the work flow for any process to reduce costs, reduce cycle times, eliminate human slips, reduce repetitive manual tasks, and provide measurement.

18. *Smooth work flow.* Yearly, monthly, weekly, and daily changes in demand often cause work flow to fluctuate widely. Many organizations staff for peak demands, rather than better distribute the demand itself. Focusing on the demand (pull) results in a smoother work flow and reduces peaks and valleys. There are many innovative supply-chain solutions available.

19. *Do tasks in parallel.* Many systems are designed so that tasks are completed in a series or linear sequence. The second task is not begun until the first task is completed, and so on. Sometimes, improvements in time and costs can be gained from designing the system to do some or all tasks in parallel. Automation lends itself well to this solution.

20. *Consider people in the same system.* Some innovative solutions are based entirely in the realm of communication, goals, and reorganization. People in different systems (departments) are usually working toward different purposes, each trying to optimize their own system. Look to the cutting-edge organizations for innovations.

21. *Use multiple processing units.* Manufacturing organizations have often gained flexibility in controlling the work flow, by creating multiple work stations, machines, processing lines, and fillers in their systems. This makes it possible to run smaller lots for special customers, minimizing the impact of maintenance and downtime, and adds flexibility to staffing. Service organizations could apply this solution to many of their offerings.

22. *Adjust to peak demand.* In direct contrast to "load leveling," accurate anticipation of peak demands may be a viable solution. This solution often requires cutting edge analytics, based on historical data. When predicted the process or service can be ramped up to temporarily meet the increased demand.

Optimize Inventory

Inventory of any type should be considered a source of waste in an organization. Inventory requires investment, storage and people to handle and keep track of it. In manufacturing organizations, inventory includes raw materials waiting to be processed, in-process inventory, and finished-good inventory. Inventory within service organizations includes the number of skilled workers available and not working. Solutions abound in the supply chain arena that can be applied quite broadly in many situations.

23. *Match inventory to predicted demand.* Excess inventory is a natural offshoot of risk aversion and results in higher costs with no improvement in performance for an organization. Creative solutions include predictive modeling

to gauge the demand, leading to replenishing inventory in an economical manner.

24. *Use pull systems.* This solution has earned its own category. In the pull system-based process, work at any particular step in the process is done only if the next step in the process is demanding the work. Only enough inputs are ordered or replenished based upon what was just used. This stands in contrast to most traditional push systems, in which work is done as long as inputs are available. A pull system is designed to match production quantities with a downstream need. This approach has applications across more than manufacturing. Pull systems are most beneficial in processes that require short cycle times and high yields.

25. *Reduce choice of features.* Reassessing market and customer demands may indicate that some features are universally added to products and services to accommodate the desires of different customers and different markets, at huge unneeded costs. Each of these features makes sense in the context of a particular customer at a particular time, but taken as a whole, they can have tremendous impact on processing cost. A review of current demand for each feature and consideration of grouping the features can allow a reduction in inventory without loss of customer satisfaction. Solutions in this context are often discovered through client or customer research.

26. *Reduce multiple brands of same items.* A desire to meet all specific customer demands has often led to its using more than one brand of any particular input or product component. When this condition occurs, inventory costs will usually be higher than necessary since a backup supply of each brand must be kept. Solutions may require research, but often require renegotiations.

Change the Work Environment

Changes to the environment in which people work, study, and live can often provide leverage for improvements in performance. As organizations try to improve quality, reduce costs, or increase the value of their products and services, technical changes are developed, tested, and implemented. Many of these technical changes do not lead to improvement because the work environment is not ready to accept or support the changes. Changing the work environment itself can be a high-leverage opportunity for making other changes more effective.

27. *Give people access to information.* Traditional organizations carefully controlled the information available to various groups of employees. Access to information is most often minimized rather than maximized. Information should be provided at or slightly above the level of the individual's decision making authority. Solutions may include not only the information availability but the modes of communication.

28. *Use proper measurements.* Throughout the process improvement movement measurement have played a critical role in focusing people on particular aspects of a business. Creative solutions can drive organizational behavior and lead to improvement throughout the organization.

29. *Take care of basics.* Fundamental problems are generally rooted in a lack of fundamental knowledge or control. These fundamentals may include the basic "101s" or they may be organization specific. Concepts like orderliness, cleanliness, discipline, and managing costs and prices are examples of such fundamentals. Continuous and creative reemphasis of the basics are essential to the ongoing health of the organization. Revisit the "Five-S's," which are at the foundation of the Japanese quality improvement effort and continue to be applicable to any organization, to this day. There are some extremely in-

novative back-to-basics solutions available today.

30. *Reduce de-motivating aspects of the pay system.* Since the mid-1940s it has been known that incentives have their proper place within an organization's performance plan. The problem is that most organizations have not listened to science and have the equation totally turned around. Solutions require some finesse, but the benefits are great. Review the organization's pay-for-performance system to ensure that the current system does not cause problems in the organization.

31. *Conduct training.* When an organization gets into trouble, one of the first areas to be down-sized is generally training. Training is basic requirement of sustained performance and the ability to make improvements. Innovative solutions abound, with many of them being low-cost, high return.

32. *32. Implement cross-training.* Cross-training means training people within an organization to be able to do multiple jobs. Such training allows for flexibility and makes changes easier. The investment required for the extra training will pay off in productivity, product quality, and cycle times.

33. *Invest more resources in improvement.* In some organizations, people spend more than a full-time job getting their required tasks completed and fighting the fires. The only changes made within their jobs are those reactions to problems or changes mandated from outside the organization. To break out of this mode, management must learn how to start investing time in developing, testing, and implementing changes that will lead to improvements and minimize the amount required to achieve a goal.

34. *Focus on core processes and purpose.* Core processes are the processes directly related to the purpose of the organization and add value to the product created. A good way to identify a core process is those things that are directly sold to an external customer. Many organizations get distracted from their core processes and lose sight of the customer. Redirecting the organization's focus through innovative means can yield high returns.

35. *Share risks.* Every business is faced with taking risks, and reaping their accompanying potential rewards or losses. DMADD is focused on reducing risks associated with decisions. Developing systems that allow all employees to identify and reduce risks, or share in the risks can lead to an increased interest in performance. Innovative solutions can include plans for sharing risks and gains include profit sharing, gain sharing, bonuses, and pay for knowledge.

36. *Emphasize natural and logical consequences.* This solution is often creating an alternative approach to traditional reward-and-punishment (R&P) systems in organizations. This means that the organization shifts its focus R&P to natural and logical consequences. Natural consequences follow from the natural order of the physical world (jumping in the water gets a person wet), while logical consequences follow from the reality of the business or social world
(If one is late for a meeting, he will not have a chance to attend). The idea of emphasizing natural and logical consequences is to get everyone to be responsible for their own behavior which is one of the talents emphasized in the 21st century workforce.

37. *Develop alliances/cooperative relationships.* Cooperative alliances optimize the interactions between the parts of a system and offer a better approach for integration of organizations. There are many organizations willing to do this.

Enhance the Producer/Customer Relationship

To benefit from improvements in quality of products and services, the customer must recognize and appreciate the improvements. Many sources for innovative ideas for improvement can come from suppliers or from the customers. Many problems in organizations exist because the organization does not understand the customer's needs, or because customers are not clear about their expectations of suppliers. There are many innovative solutions available to interface the organization with the customer.

38. *Listen to customers.* It is easy for the organization to get caught up in its internal issues and forget why they are in business. Time should be invested on a regular basis in processes that listen to the customers. Not only is this a solution, it is also a source of improvement opportunities.

39. *Coach customers to use the product/service.* Many innovations exist around coaching and training customers. Quality problems can and do increase their costs because of their lack of knowledge about the intricacies of the product or service. Many organizations have increased the value of their products and services by developing innovative means of working with customers on the use of the products they buy.

40. *Focus on the outcome to a customer.* Rather than an inward focus upon activities, shift to a focus on the outcome (the product or service) generated by your organization. This often requires reorganizing people, departments, and processes in a way that best serves the customer, paying particular attention to the product/customer interfaces. This change concept can also be described as "backward development," "reverse engineering," or "begin with the end in mind."

41. *Use of a coordinator.* A coordinator's role is to manage supplier/producer/customer relationship. A well-known example is engaging an expeditor as someone who focuses on ensuring adequate supplies of materials and equipment or who goes one step further and coordinates the flow of materials through the organization. The coordinator role can be expanded and defined in any way to meet the needs of this important set of relationships.

42. *Reach agreement on expectations.* Competitive marketing often leads to customer dissatisfaction, because they feel that they have not received the products or services they were led to expect as a result of advertising, special promotions, and promises by the marketing and sales groups. These groups should be included in all discussions related with production capabilities. Innovative marketing and sales methods abound across the information highway. They can be leveraged into almost every organization's product or service. Follow the leaders.

43. *Outsource for "free."* Creative solutions exist in getting suppliers to perform additional functions for the customer with little or no increase in the price to the customer. Involving suppliers in the problem solving often leads to creative solutions that already exist. Many times the supplier is willing to do this task for "free" in order to secure ongoing business with you, their customer.

44. *Optimize level of inspection.* Aligning the level of inspection which is appropriate for a process is critical with minimizing operational costs. All products will eventually undergo some type of inspection, possibly by the user. There are many options for inspection at any given point in the process/supply chain. Many of these solutions are automated, because they're 100 percent repetitive.

45. *Work with suppliers.* The most significant level of process control comes from controlling inputs. Engaging with suppliers and using their technical knowledge can often reduce the cost of using their products or services. Suppliers may even have ideas on how to make changes in a company's process that will improve the product or service.

Manage Time

Cutting cycle time is a common strategy for improving any organization. An organization can gain a competitive advantage by reducing the time to develop new products, waiting times for the delivery of product or services, and for all internal functions and processes. Because this has been repeatedly addressed by many organizations, many creative solutions exist.

46. *Reduce setup or startup time.* Many innovations exist to reduce startup time. Creative adaptation of existing methods can often cut time in half.

47. *Set up timing to use discounts.* At the core of this strategy is flexible processing. The planning and timing of many activities can be coordinated to take advantage of savings and discounts that are available to them, resulting in a reduction of operating costs. These are creative applications of "what if?"

48. *Optimize maintenance.* Unscheduled maintenance loses time, volume, and quality. There are many innovative preventive and predictive maintenance strategies available. Suppliers can assist with proper design elements and a thorough the study of historical data, aligned with an efficient maintenance program can be designed to keep equipment in production with a minimum of downtime for maintenance. An often overlooked element within a production and service environment is the people. Like a machine, they periodically require maintenance, such as training, time off, etc. Creative ap-

plication of discoveries can boost production, service, and quality.

49. *Extend specialists' time.* Organizations employ specialists who have specific skills or knowledge, but not all of their work duties utilize these skills or knowledge. Eliminating those tasks that are not within their skill set and the innovative use of their specific skills can improve organizational performance significantly.

50. *Reduce wait time.* Many innovative systems and methods exist to reduce customer wait time. A true end to end view of the customer experience with your organization is often alarming, but acts as the catalyst for real customer impacting improvements.

Manage Variation

Most of the traditional quality and cost reduction efforts have focused on the reduction of process or service variation. Reducing variation improves the predictability of outcomes and allows an organization to better control its operating expenses. Many innovations exist to deal with process or system variation. Do not push the limits until your organization has a strong foundation built. Business process management (BPM) and statistical process control (SPC) is constantly being improved upon. Yet there remain three basic approaches to address variation issues: reducing the variation, compensating for the variation, or exploiting the variation.

51. *Standardization (creating a formal process).* Standardization is a critical element to consistent and stable performance. The use of standards has both negative and bureaucratic (controlling) connotations to many people, along with positive and liberating ones. Standardization is a basic tactic in reducing variation in a system. As basic as it is, it also has many innovative applications.

52. *Stop tampering.* Removing the ability to adjust or "tweak" a process oftentimes requires innovative control solutions. This solution also requires measures and monitoring systems to ensure that the system does not return to its prior state.

53. *Develop operational definitions.* Although not an innovative concept to organizations that have had previous contact with process improvement efforts, concise definitions and clarification of expectations is important. Significant reduction in process or service variation can be obtained with a common understanding of concepts commonly used in the transaction of business. Eliminate the "I thought you meant" excuse.

54. *Improve predictions.* Innovative methods for forecasting exist and are constantly being refined. Many organizations "reinvent the wheel" each time a forecast is required. Establishing a cutting edge technology and engaging a specialist, pays-off in high returns, to organizations that require this to maintain market share and grow.

55. *Develop contingency plans.* Many organizations are hard pressed to meet the daily needs of production and service. This puts alternative processing planning at the very bottom of the priority list. Innovative methods and other organizations are constantly springing up to help established organizations meet the alternative needs.

56. *Sort product into grades.* Innovative and creative techniques exist to take full advantage of incoming, process, and output variations in products. Sorting the materials and even people (based upon skill) into different grades can minimize the variation within a grade and maximize the variation between grades, thereby maximizing profitability

57. *Desensitize.* Innovative marketing can help control some types of variation that heretofore were impossible to control. This change strategy focuses on desensitizing the effect of variation rather than wasting effort on attempting to reduce the incidence of variation.

58. *Exploit variation.* In some instances it is sometimes unclear how variation can be reduced or eliminated. This change strategy looks for ways to use it to the advantage of the product or service.

Design Systems to Avoid Mistakes

It is inevitable that human beings will make mistakes; the probability of a mistake increases as the number of people in a system increases or the number of interactions of people within the system increases. It is purely a numbers game. There are numerous innovations to reduce interaction and or people within processes. Begin searches around error-proofing. Many organizations have created systems using technology. These are off the shelf and can be easily applied to almost every circumstance.

59. *Use reminders.* Automated reminder systems abound. Creative and innovated methods to avoid the mistakes created by forgetting to do something pay high dividends for little investment.

60. *Use differentiation.* Errors often result when individuals are forced to deal with situations or materials that look nearly the same. Many innovations have arisen to address these error types.

61. *Use constraints.* An entire methodology based its success on the identification and elimination of process or service constraints. An innovative solution set turns the table and uses constraints to improve process or service performance.

62. *Use affordances.* The opposite of a constraint is an affordance. In direct contrast to a constraint, which limits actions, an affordance provides visual or other sensory prompting for the actions that should be performed. When a process or product is designed to lead the user to perform the correct actions, fewer mistakes occur.

Focus on the Product or Service

Most of the change strategies in the other categories address the way that a process or service is performed; many innovations exist to improve the actual product or service. This strategy set consists of innovation recommendations that focus on the changes to a product or service that do not naturally fit into any of the other groupings.

63. *Mass-customize.* Many innovative organizations have developed ways to make common products custom. Marketing insights indicate that consumers perceive quality increases as the product or service is customized to the customer's unique circumstances. Most consumers pay more or wait longer for these customized offerings than for a mass-produced version. Seek out these organizations and leverage their lessons.

64. *Offer the product or service anytime.* The global economy now necessitates the need for a 24-hour operation. In the past, products and services were available only at certain times. Such constraints almost always detract from some aspect of quality. Look to innovative organizations, products and services that have broken that mold.

65. *Offer the product or service anyplace.* A new demand of the virtual world is convenience. To make a product or service more convenient, it must be released from the constraints of space. Innovative organizations have made their offerings available anyplace. Look to these organizations for ideas to change availability.

66. *Emphasize intangibles.* Many products and services are purchased and used for reasons beyond the utility for which they were designed. Identifying those utilities and emphasizing them can lead to new markets and innovative uses for existing products and services.

67. *Influence or take advantage of fashion trends.* Many innovative and cutting-edge companies stay attuned to fads and trends and react quickly and effectively. A continuous monitoring of these companies can lead to interesting discoveries and unimaginable innovations. Some organizations go as far as promoting specific trends. These should always be considerations within your sales and marketing organizations.

68. *Reduce the number of components.* One of the earlier strategies was to reducing handoffs. In that same vein, reducing the complexity of a product or service by reducing the number of component parts is a way to simplify a product. Innovation often includes getting down to exactly what the customer is buying.

69. *Disguise minor defects and problems.* This should not be confused with real product or service flaws, just those things that divert the customer attention from the real value. Some innovative organizations have addressed inconsequential product and service defects by covering them rather than replacing them. Super-extended warranties or thicker paint are great examples of meeting and exceeding customer needs with little additional cost.

70. *Differentiate product using quality dimensions.* Nothing improves customer satisfaction more than matching their "must-haves" and "delighters" with the product or service they ordered. Quality matching is determined using marketing and customer research. Innovative organizations arise continuously that conduct customer research can provide an understanding of customer's needs and wants.

The detail presented over these 70 strategies can help direct the "Key Phrase" search and the solutions tree. This activity should be conducted in two ways. The first exercise of the concepts should look for direct application and search for ideas. The second exercise of the concepts is the exact inverse. It should eliminate those that have no application whatsoever and search those that were not eliminated. Along the path of the search, many new solutions will be found. These should be added to the solutions tree for subsequent decompositions.

Process/Project Model

Of nearly equal importance to the solutions tree in DMADD is a "process/project" model. The model provides the practitioner with the ability to confirm the baseline or existing process and to test the various options that are discovered along the journey. In the perfect DMADD world, a representative model exists for each of the organization's core processes. Recognizing the fact that few organizations have developed this luxury, we'll discuss the basic requirements of the DMADD supporting model.

Although presented at this point in the overall effort, this should not lead the reader to wait until this point in the project. It should be started as soon as possible. This is recommended because modeling is often arduous and time-consuming. As previously emphasized, the value derived from modeling is directly related to the amount of time spent developing a representative system and the data that feeds it. My advice is that it should be started no later than this phase in the individual project effort.

There are no specific examples of a process/project model presented or recommended. This is because this activity varies significantly, based upon the complexity of the project and/or the accuracy or confidence demands of the organization. In its most simplistic form, the model could simply be a huge dataset with information representing all of the various iterations found in the solution tree. Then testing or modeling is simply a matter of a "what if?" type of data segmentation. This means that one parses out the individual activities that represent what the process would look like if the process performed one with a certain set of characteristics.

On the opposite end of the spectrum, the model could be a specialized software application that is populated with actual process data. Whatever the case, it is important to obtain the organizations' buy-in and support of the model being utilized. This model fills an important role in the decision-making process and ensuring support will speed this activity.

Whatever modeling methodology is chosen, it should be established and uniformly utilized throughout the project. If the model is changed all prior scenarios should be re-run to alleviate any chance of arguments for a previously eliminated option.

A required process model is unique to the DMADD methodology. Its purpose is to replicate the expected outcomes of the effort and keep it focused on delivering the results. The model drives the final decision and then acts as the standard for closure. If the effort performs as the model projected, the project is closed. If the results are less than expected, the differences are reconciled and corrective actions are taken. If the results are better than expected, the project does not simply close, as it would in many of the other methodologies; rather, the differences are again reconciled, and the model is adjusted and the reasons for the differences are investigated until they are understood. This sets the stage for future improvements to both the modeling effort and the organization on a whole.

Close attention should be paid not only to the control and consistency of the input variables and the subsequent effect on the outputs, but also on all of the related characteristics found within the C/E/I activity. Taking all of the other characteristics into consideration allows for the calculation of the "Impact" portion of the equation in the C/E/I activity. At this point, one sees that this activity is directly linked to and feeds and/or updates the C/E/I. Elementary practitioners often fail to update the C/E/I with these discoveries and accurate total impacts are not communicated.

Although the information in this section is brief, do not underestimate the power of an accurate and powerful model. It actually becomes a safe playground in which numerous "what if?" scenarios can be developed and tested without any organizational impact.

I have not been with an organization where an individual has not become enamored with modeling and stepped up with a passion for this exercise. As expected, that person becomes the organization's subject matter expert and that talent is leveraged into every project. If time and money allows, I have focused that individual on modeling and when they are not working on specific project models, their talent is leveraged into creating an organization-wide set of models. Not only does this effort create a proactive library of models, for future projects, it also maintains an interconnected set that eliminates the issues resulting from the creation of models by multiple individuals. Moreover, comprehensive modeling directly supports the C/E/I efforts. As I had previously noted, many organizations do not recognize the full impact of their seemingly isolated and internal changes. Comprehensive models can be used to support isolating root causes and then when solutions are recommended, the full extent of impact of the change. This helps ensure that the changes within the organization have direct impact to the overall bottom line of the organization, and that the real return on investments are realized.

EPO Update

This will become a redundant topic from this point forward. Every phase requires an update and presentation of the executive project overview (EPO). The practitioner should remember that an update to the pre-existing document is not sufficient. It must be presented and discussed and no further project activity is conducted until all of the decision-makers have approved of the status and agree with all of the activities of the previous phase.

The EPO used at this point is the same document found in the initial phases of the project. In fact, the initial EPO is used as the starting point. If some standard and general guidelines in its development are used, the EPO is a smooth and brief activity. They are:

- Any changes from the original document are noted in a colored font different from the original font color

- All changes of significance are hyper-linked to detailed documentation, which is reviewed, as needed, by the decision-makers

- Any concerns are addressed prior to continued activity

- Upon approval, the font color reverts to the original document font color

It has been found that making the original font color black and the update color red seems to work best. This is a matter of preference, but once this has been chosen it should be standardized across all DMADD activities.

Nothing should be taken on an individual's word or perception. Everything must have support documentation. This is not to underplay the competence of the leader, but shows the thoroughness of the initiative and it also dispels and challenges that may arise when the effort switches from a data driven effort to a emotional charged challenge.

All stakeholders must have their say and concerns must be addressed prior to continued activity. This proactively addresses unintentional subversion of the project through passive resistance. This also puts an onus on the team leader—whose charge it is to keep the project moving—to be proactive in communication and have numerous meetings before the formal EPO meeting. It also puts a responsibility on individual stakeholder to decide rather than stalemate an effort. It does this by documenting and broadly communicating the concern and required effort for resolution. This single "DMADD rule of engagement" makes all the difference in project success.

When issues are resolved, the font color reverts to the base color. This simple change often deters individuals from revisiting issues by its subtle reminder that it "was asked and answered!"

Chapter 6

DMADD – Analyze

"Every master knows that the materials teach the artist."
—Ilya Ehrenburg

DELIVERABLES

1. Validation of Required Deliverables
2. Solutions Tree (Levels 2 – 4)
3. Cause/Effect/Impact
4. Opportunity/Effort/Risk
5. Comparative Solution Analysis
6. "To Be" SIPOC
7. "To Be" Process Map
8. Process Model
9. Solution Recommendation Finalization
10. Executive Project Overview (EPO)

PHASE GOALS:

- Revalidation of the project deliverables
- Update of all effected previous activities

- A Solution recommendation
- The proposed documentation related to the recommendation
- Executive Approval and Support of the recommendation

This is where it is all pulled together. The most difficult part of this effort is trying to describe that effort in a linear fashion. The last two phases in DMADD are anything but linear. Rather, they are quite integrated, and many times changes or discoveries will force the practitioner to briefly go back and update the previous steps. After all of the initial work, there is a temptation to drive to a solution and allow an answer to drive the project, without all of the pertinent information. This is generally a result of impatience and time constraints. It is the sponsor's responsibility to ward off the wolves and provide the DMADD team with sufficient breathing room so that the right decisions can be made and driven. The unspoken but very apparent goal of DMADD is to drive the risk out of the decision-making equation. This is accomplished through a series of linked activities. Linkages are essential, and continuous updating of the previous activities should not be ignored. There is a huge price related to efforts that do not keep the project continuously updated. That price is a risky decision. When this happens, risk rears its ugly head and the result is less-than-amazing results. The Initial Solution established at the project onset becomes the initial hypothesis (in the traditional sense), and the initial modeling inputs in the DMADD perspective. Next, the critical drivers from the C/E/I are tested against the solution, and finally the model created in the prior phase is tested and validated. When these initial (transitional) activities are completed it is an opportune time to confirm the original project expectations.

Validations of Required Deliverables

Whether the project follows the path of traditional process improvement strategies or those of DMADD, there are often discoveries made during their course that change sponsor or decision-maker perspectives. Process improvement professionals do not ask the following question often enough: "Are we still chasing the same things?" This actually needs to become a routine. Project failures are often rooted in a lack of communication. Even though we are keenly aware of this, we need to put a formal communication exercise around this and it needs to become a habit.

Up to this point, no specific document has been required to validate the deliverables. It has been embedded in the straight talk, the charter, the EPO and the exit strategy. These were used to affirm the issues and confirm the expectations from many different directions to catch idiosyncratic differences. Although it may appear redundant, all of the documents that contain the related information are consolidated, reviewed for consistency and affirmed in the following document. If the EPO has been utilized as previously presented, there should be no surprises.

One of the purposes of the EPO is to maintain constant communication and reaffirm the project's expectations. Ensuring that the entire project and its documentation reflect the latest updates to the EPO is important. There should never be conflicting numbers in a project, even if everyone agrees that what was on the old is old and no longer relevant. Those agreements are quickly forgotten at a quarterly budget review meeting.

I can not over-emphasize that one can never verify what is expected of a project too often. During the define phase, the current performance and required performance characteristics were initially consolidated to make the compelling case for the project. Before any additional activity within the effort, the expected deliverable in terms of Δ (delta, or net change) is confirmed with the project sponsor to ensure that there are absolutely no misunderstandings between any of the stakeholders.

This information should have been captured in the exit strategy. This puts a beginning and an ending to the project. It is important to maintain absolute integrity across all documents of the project, between the charter and the exit strategy. The project is simply a matter of connecting those two documents. At this point all of the expectations should merge into one document. An example of the basic deliverable consolidation document follows.

Project Deliverables

Output Characteristic	Current	Required	Δ
Volume			
Time			
Quality			
Cost			

Project Sponsor _____   Date _____

Project Leader _____   Date _____

There may multiple output characteristics or other objectives associated with the project. Alter the document accordingly, capturing each and every expectation. These will come into play as decisions are finalized. Another caution: Do not allow the appearance of redundancy to justify skipping this step. Stakeholders and team leaders should never hear the comment, "I thought you were going to fix..."

Solutions Tree (Levels 2 – 4)

The Solutions Tree (Level 1), which was created in the previous project phase, established the baseline (the do-nothing) alternative and the initial solution. At that juncture, there was no real way of determining if the proposed solution is really the best resolution or just a better alternative. It just was a solution. The search and research then identified numerous solutions to the issue in whole or in part. These are added to the solutions tree at this point on the level one tree. You can see that the work now begins!

The subsequent levels (2 through 4) decompose all of the

aforementioned solutions (including the do-nothing alternative) into lower levels of detail, to ascertain their true costs and values. The following diagrams are not intended to be an actual solutions tree, but a representation of the concepts. Many solutions trees are very complex and, if fully printed, can and often do occupy an entire wall. Attention to detail is a project leader's best friend during this activity.

Level 2

The Level 1 solutions tree is often referred to as the solution level tree. Its purpose is to capture the various alternatives afforded to an organization, in addressing the issue. The Level 2 solutions tree is called the "requirement level" tree. Knowing that there is a specific set of output requirements, this tree actually captures the "what is needed" in order to make the solution viable and the subsequent effect on time, volume, quality, and cost, in each of the categories of people, process and technology. The diagram shows decomposition for process only. The same decomposition would occur for people and technology.

Level 2

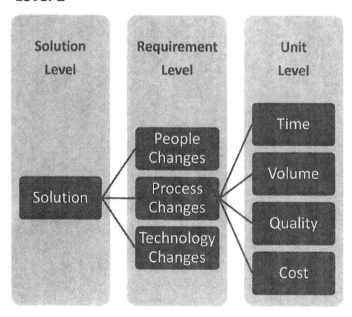

Level 3

The Level 3 solutions tree is referred to as the unit level tree. This tree systematically decomposes all of the characteristics of a processing unit. The diagram below only addresses the volume characteristic. Identical decomposition should occur for the other three characteristics.

Level 3

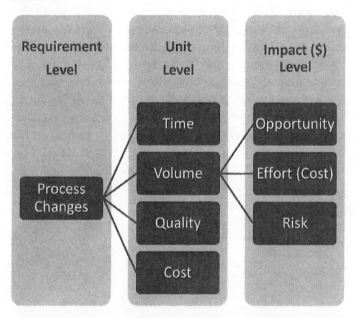

Level 4

The Level 4 solutions tree is referred to as the impact level tree. At this point, the impacts for each solution are re-composed with the following equation:

IMPACT = (Opportunity – Effort) X Risk

A few critical components are missing (hidden) with this analysis. If we return for a moment to the C/E/I analysis, we remember that for every effect, there is an impact to every branch or bone on the impact side of the equation. That means that the six branches (man, materials, methods, machinery, Mother Nature, and management) will all be affected to some extent by a change. The logical affects are negative, neutral or positive. There are many details to this analysis, but the value derived from this thoroughness well outweighs the costs.

This sets the stage for a realistic comparison of each of the solutions. It is easy to see that if any information is missing from a solution (or if the information is inaccurate) the solution quickly falls out of contention for viability.

Level 4

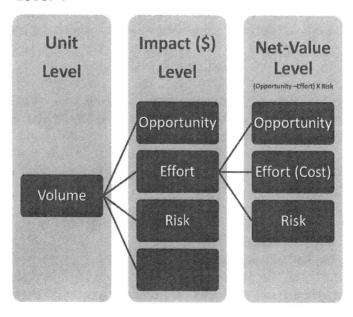

Recomposition

Adaption is the key word at this juncture in the methodology. It should become apparent (except for extreme cases in which DMADD is not applicable) that reinventing the wheel is not necessary. Utilizing the details compiled during re-composition within the analyze phase creates a "best-fit" and comprehensive solution set. We are often preconditioned to believe that a single solution provides the answer. That belief often leads to sub-optimization. Creativity is essential during the recomposition activity and the assembly of the solution. Pick and choose, like you are at a buffet. Combine aspects of the solutions presented and make the optimum solution.

Recomposition leads to and often forces the first non-linear activity. Adjustments made to the presentation of the single solution set will affect the C/E/I analysis. Do not skip reviewing this document and make changes as necessary.

Cause/Effect/Impact

Earlier in the project, the emphasis within this activity was on populating the causes and effects. When the project has progressed to a point that the team is assured that the causes and effects are accurate and comprehensive, the emphasis shifts to the impacts. Impacts are simply defined as the total cost associated with any effect. Calculating cost associated with the effect (impact) and connecting that cost with the causes puts the project into the proper organizational perspective; this effort either finalizes its justification or kills the project entirely. That is why it is important to gain agreement on the deliverables early in this phase. Comprehensive analysis is required to ensure that when alternate solutions are brought into the decision scheme, they are all on the same decision scheme. In simpler terms, it's comparing apples to apples.

This is the point in which the cost of poor quality (CoPQ) is tied to impacts. The more comprehensive the CoPQ analysis the more valid and substantial justification for the change is gathered. The old saying "the bottom line is the bottom line" becomes one of the major drivers of the decision-making process. When organizations realize the true costs associated with an issue, the risks associated with "not doing something" grow exponentially and a decision is made. On the other hand, if the true CoPQ is minimal, there may be other costs, such as a cost to the organization related to reduced time and effort. Baseline impacts and expected project impact calculations are critical to good organizational decision-making. Most organizations do not have the luxury of making risky decisions or simply making decisions at the whim of an individual. C/E/I combined with the CoPQ guide quick, informed and risk-reduced decision-making, especially when linked to and tested with a representative model.

Opportunity/Effort/Risk

Traditional decision-making methodologies focused upon the opportunity afforded by the proposed change and the cost or effort required to effect the change. In DMADD, the two-dimensional opportunity/effort matrix is expanded into three dimensions by the inclusion of risk. Risk is defined as the chance that the proposed solution will not have the same effect in the current situation as experienced or reported by those found in the searches and presented within the model.

Decompose and re-compose, mentioned earlier in the solutions tree section of this chapter, is a problem-solving tactic that has followed me throughout my career and it is embedded throughout DMADD. This tactic revolves around the activities that work to decompose the issue, the recommended solution, and the related process into its critical few components. It then re-composes them and the suggestions into a viable solution set. This tactic is discussed in detail in the DMADD training. Volumes can be written on this subject alone, and its effectiveness requires attention to detail. Our practitioners are constantly under the guidance of individuals who have had significant experience to ensure that no critical aspects of the decomposition or the recomposition are missed.

The O/E/R is well suited for decomposition/recomposition, and it sets the stage for use of the same tactic with the solutions tree. The crux of the analysis in DMADD is the alignment of the decomposed issues to the detailed effects and impacts and decomposed and re-composed solutions. It thoroughly pursues and clarifies the answer to the questions:

- What is the real issue?
- What are you really proposing to do?
- Is it within our risk limitations?
- Will it do what we need it to do?
- Is the cost of change worth it?"

Keeping these questions in mind during the analyze phase of the project will drive it in the right direction.

This requires an accurate C/E/I, a complete solutions tree and an O/E/R. Up to this point, the tree was used to document the issue, create a performance baseline (through the do-nothing alternative) and clarify the proposed solution (as option #1). From henceforth the tree will be used to decompose the improvement strategy and suggest and/or confirm alternative strategies. This along with alignment with existing population segmentations will create a list of plausible alternatives.

Comparative Solutions Analysis

Even with the best projects, there are a few iterations and updates between the solutions tree and the C/E/I. Many practitioners have complained, "When is this going to end?" referring to the circular activity. Assuming that the alternatives have been exhausted and documented, this the point in the project when all of the previous activities begin to bear fruit. It can not be over-emphasized that a comprehensive set of alternatives generated via the solutions tree are critical. Internet searches and Triz searches should be discussed at length. This single most important piece of advice for a project leader and the sponsor is to let the data talk. Data gleaned during the various searches is consolidated into meaningful groups. The groupings are interpreted and changed into information. The information is then applied to the organization and converted into insight. These insights reduce organizational risk.

Some traditional practitioner may argue that DMADD lacks

scientific integrity at this point. To address this, the methodology has morphed slightly. There are two paths that can be taken at this point in the methodology.

* The Regression path – This varies the "X" components of the equation to see if the anticipated results meet expectations.

* The Modeling path, in which models are created to validate assumptions made within the solutions tree.

In either case, the organizational data collides with the project data, resulting in the aforementioned insights. An interesting traditional statistical concept is challenged herein. DMADD's analysis success is defined significantly differently from what the DMAIC practitioner is accustomed to.

Traditional analytic confidence is indirectly expressed by the p-value. Without going into long boring details of this argument, the p-value is the amount of risk that the organization is willing to assume related to the accuracy of the findings. Unless population data is utilized, there will always be a risk associated with the conclusions. There is absolutely nothing wrong with this strategy, yet all but the most astute statisticians have to test one variable at a time. This is a time-consuming ordeal, and something that 21st century organizations can not afford. In simplistic terms, in "testing one factor at a time" data is held constant, analyzed, and the p-value derived, then success or failure of the analysis is then declared. Many practitioners will argue that multiple regressions resolves this issue, but then variable interactions come into play and a whole new set of positive and negative issues can arise. This will continue to be discussed and final resolution is probably not possible. From a DMADD standpoint, it really doesn't matter. If one's confidence is in regression and advanced analytics, great. That path can be also applied to DMADD.

Where DMADD is unique is that within the analytical phase, the drivers are varied and an optimized solution is created within the model. One can easily see that the preferred analytical method is through modeling and adjustment, rather than the "best fit" found in regression. Rather than submitting the organization to a static "p," which is interpreted into a range of accuracy upon which they make their decisions, the best alternative is determined and efforts continue until the level of performance is achieved.

In segmentation modeling, more or less of the affected population is removed or added until the solution is optimized. Once the confidence levels (intervals) are established, the insights are communicated in terms of ranges rather than a single number. I have never liked a single number commitment. Except in extreme cases they were always incorrect, being somewhat more or less than the number projects (yet within my confidence intervals). My normal strategy is to place the organization need at the lower estimate and the estimated performance range beyond that. In that case, an organization can expect that the project will deliver to their needs at minimum and can only exceed their requirements over the course of time.

Once all of the impacts for all of the potential solutions are compared to each other, the decision is relatively easy. In fact, the need for a decision is eliminated. There should be multiple comparisons, a unit comparison, a dollar comparison, and, finally, a net comparison. In every case, the individual elements are compared in two ways: the median expected performance and the range of each respective element.

More often than not, a solution rises to the top of the list, and there are no concerns to be addressed. Other times, more work (analysis and modeling) is required. Either result is a success. If the latter situation occurs, remember to re-negotiate the project time expectations. Remaining focused on DMADD's strength, which is finding the best solution for issue, will carry much weight as it gains internal organizational acceptance.

"To Be" SIPOC

In most cases, one solution or solution set will rise to the top of the decision list. In rare instances more than one alternative may appear viable. In either case the next two activities are important— even though their roles change, depending upon the status of the solution. The SIPOC —which you will recall is a shortened form of supplier/input/process/output/customer—

acts as the basic documentation for the proposed solution or as a viability/reality check in the case of multiple solutions. Developing the "to be" SIPOC at this stage in the project sets up the initial documentation for the solution, the project communication plan and the comprehensive project plan. Both will be discussed in the next chapter.

The important emphasis should be on accuracy. This is not another check mark. The project leader should put as much time as is needed to develop the new SIPOC. It should consistently match the proposed solution—and in the case of multiple solutions, each should show the differences. These differences act as reality or viability checks. Oftentimes it becomes apparent that one solution, although viable theoretically does not make sense when looked at from an application point of view. The simplicity of the SIPOC makes these differences visible.

"To Be" Process Map

In order to implement an organizational change or a process change, the practitioner needs to know exactly what needs to be changed. This may sound self-evident, but many projects fail because the team did not fully understand everything that was required to execute the change. Many "shoot from the hip" or "fly by the seat of the pants" organizations do this. They make the decision and go! DMADD can not tolerate this organizational strategy. A comprehensive understanding minimizes risk of failure. Developing a "to be" process map and comparing it to the existing map, should make it very apparent what changes are required. This comparative information can help drive an executive decision, feed the communication and project plan, and pre-populate the required documentation.

Process Model

At this point, the process model established in the previous phase is utilized to test the alternative solution and solution sets. Depending on the model type chosen, this may be an arduous task or a simple matter. The data obtained from the model can be used to adjust the solution sets and/or the "to be" SIPOC and the "to be" Process Map. Both of these tools/documents are also use to build or adjust the model. Also providing information to the model is the C/E/I document. These documents, along with other pieces of information, converge and prove to the organization in a low-risk way which of the alternatives are the best, and what the new world will look like. This reduces the level of surprise at the time of actual implementation to awe related to how reality was replicated in the modeling world.

Solution Recommendation Finalization/Approval

If all has progressed as presented, the solution or solution set is ready to be finalized. If the communication plan has been working, approval is simply a formality. But even though it is a formality, it needs to be documented. The solution and the antici-pated impacts should exactly match the exit strategy. If it doesn't the two need to be brought into agreement. This activity also feeds the project plan at both the high level and lower levels. An example of a solution finalization/approval document follows. As with previously presented documents, this can be adjusted to meet the needs of the organization. It is important to ensure alignment of this document with the charter, the straight talk," and the exit strategy. It is a great place for the project sponsor to check to see if the documentation has been updated as required by DMADD practitioners.

Solution Recommendation and Finalization

Proposed Solution

Anticipate d Impact(s) – Narrative:
Time -   Volume -   Quality -   Operational Cost -   CoPQ –   Net Impact -

Charter and Exit Strategy Alignment -

Approvals
Project Sponsor _____   Team Leader _____   Executive (if Required) _____   PI Leader _____

After gaining full approval, the final step is to update the EPO and communicate the approval event. Because the project sponsor and all of the relevant decision-makers have been involved in this step, the emphasis should be on celebrating a successful decision. Normally at this point in the project, the team is nearing exhaustion. A lift in enthusiasm is definitely in order. It is not time to cancel the EPO meeting. In fact, this meeting is one of the most important ones. Toward the end of the EPO update, the vote of confidence is in order and often needed. Closing the analyze phase on a high note is a great investment. This often runs contrary to many management philosophies, in that they do not want to reward their subordinates halfway through the project.

The analyze phase of DMADD focuses efforts on ascertaining the best solution or set of solutions and reducing the associated risk related to those decisions. It must be emphasized that the DMADD is more mathematical than inferential and statistical. Many hold that statistics is a science of facts, when in fact it is an inexact science of prediction. DMADD is designed to ensure that the proposed alternatives and the experienced results will closely match what was forecast within the model.

Chapter 7

DMADD – Develop

*"Intelligence recognizes what has happened.
Genius recognizes what will happen."*
—John Ciardi

DELIVERABLES

1. Project Plan
2. Pilot
3. Verification of Measures
4. The Soft Side
5. Executive project overview (EPO)

PHASE GOALS:

- A Comprehensive project plan for the delivery of the accepted solution
- Verification of existing measurement system and/or the creation of new performance measures
- Executive project overview – Approval to deliver

From the onset of the project, each phase of DMADD becomes progressively less demanding, building upon the work of the prior phases. This easing of demands is by design and is intended to get the project on a roll, then increasing the project's velocity and finally creating a condition of unavoidable success. The Develop stage will pass quickly and is (proverbially) missed if one blinks. Although not specifically noted, it is important that all of the previous documentation and activities be updated with the latest discoveries and insights. The terms "fact" and "accuracy" are relative ones, and quite dynamic. What is known to be a "fact" at present may be totally wrong tomorrow due to some discovery. The DMADD practitioner never allows the project documentation to be outdated, inaccurate, or contain misleading information. "I'll update it later" is not in our practitioner's vocabulary or behavior set.

During sponsor training, project leaders and sponsors are directed to make periodic, random, unannounced checks of the documentation for maintenance. Although not presented in this book, there is a document that we utilize to ensure dynamic updates. This unspoken and ongoing project deliverable is important to the credibility and general success of the project as well as the overall organizational acceptance of the methodology.

The Project Plan

At the core of this stage of DMADD, is a project plan, the comprehensive set of the components required to make the effective and lasting change. Many times project plans fall short of the real needs related to the effort. Most often, these projects and the related plan are myopic. These types of plans and efforts focus specifically on delivering what was being asked for, rather than making what had been asked for effective. This is the reason that the word "comprehensive" was used as the first deliverable. In order to be comprehensive, a project must address the fact that change is impacted in three general categories:

- People changes – Human competency changes such as training, skill sets, mind sets and/or behavior sets

- Process changes – May include equipment, buildings, measurements, sequence changes, flow changes, or management changes

- Technology changes – May include new support changes, hardware, and/or software

A comprehensive plan will address the required changes and the activities to achieve the overall objectives. I am often asked why I specifically say "changes." The semi-serious response is that if a change is not required, why do anything? The fact of the matter is that the most effective plans comprehensively address all of the required changes, but only the required changes.

That having been said, the format of the plan is irrelevant. As with many of the other exercises and documents, it is more important that the organization sees them in a format that they understand and accept, as long as they contain the critical pieces of information. It is therefore safe to assume that a majority of the deliverables will resemble those in a comprehensive project management initiative. Any project management system will work as long as the aforementioned elements are contained within it.

At this point, it is necessary to revisit the risk side of the O/E/R equation to address decision-maker concerns. This is really what the project plan is about. Up to this point DMADD has focused upon accurately identifying the cause, the effect and the impact. Risk has been somewhat conjectured. Now this characteristic needs to be controlled and the organization needs to be able to trust that the project will have, at minimum, the risk that was projected and used to make the decision. This means that the project plan will avert all risk and its related effort will deliver the desired results. As a result, the emphasis must be on accurately identifying the required components of change. In a sense, the project plan is the risk mitigation plan.

Pilot

During the initial development of the project plan, there may be a need for a pilot or a proof of concept test. When conducted and the actual performance (results) of the test are compared to what was forecasted in the model match, it is a definite boost to the methodology's credibility. If the results do not match, breathe a huge sigh of relief and adjust the risk-decision variable and/or then the project plan. The focus must be on assuring the organization that the desired results can be delivered. In doing so, the risk characteristic of O/E/R is controlled or mitigated. At this point, many will ask, "Why the risk?"

Business can be distilled to a series of decisions and delivery on those decisions. The single element that stops the transition from concept to delivery is the risk. This is the business model and a DMADD effort parallels this concept. The beauty is that it takes an organization down a path of the best business decisions. In the most basic sense, it identifies the opportunities, assesses the efforts, and finally controls or eliminates the risk. The relentless focus on these elements sets DMADD apart from the traditional process improvement methodologies.

In this context, DMADD should be taught as the management methodology. As previously stated, if a business is in a position of making a decision, it probably does not have sufficient information—and that condition is a good indicator that the analyze phase is not yet complete. Stated another way, there should be one option or solution at the onset of the develop phase, and it should have relatively been a no-brainer. Reducing the list to a single self-evident option makes business decision making quite simple.

As a side note, time constraints and impatience may drive a hasty decision and allows risk to permeate the decision-making process. This results in compromises. There are good compromises and poor ones. A compromise of customer requirements is a bad one; a compromise of margin that serves a customer better is a good one. The optimum solution is a win/win, one in which all pertinent voices are met or benefit from the solution. This is the answer that should be sought. It is the Holy Grail of process improvement, and especially of DMADD. Unlike the Holy Grail, it is an achievable goal. An astute solution meets all of the needs of the various demands (the six voices) and is possible for those who take the time and effort to find it. In actuality, all of this should have been accomplished in the previous stages. At this point, the project planner knows specifically what success looks like. This phase makes making what we need a reality and doing it with little or no risk.

The keys to success in this phase are the use of the tried and true project management tools. It was previously noted that Triz is a separate and stand-alone session. DMADD training is also supplemented with a one-day session called Project Management (PM) Lite. This session takes the practitioner from "a dream and a mess," to a comprehensive Gantt-based project plan. Since project management is quite standard and available in most all organizations, the review of the required activities will be kept to a minimum. The specific PM Lite activities include:

- A Project-specific straight talk

- Activity/Definition/Sequencing (ADS)

- Inter-relationship analysis and diagram

- Work breakdown structure (WBS)

- Detail project plan (Linked Outline)

- Gantt charting

- Status reporting – EPO supplemental reporting

A brief editorial comment: Many project management activities appear to exist to protect the project manager or provide authority where none exists. Rid the organization of these activities. They are a waste of valuable time and resources. Project managers do not need to spend time in "cover-your-backside" activities; they need to be focused on delivery. Whatever project management activities are required within this project, work to ensure that they fully support the delivery of the solution.

Another consideration for the sponsor to make is assigning an expert project manager at this juncture. There is no replacement for great project management. A good PI practitioner would gladly co-lead the project.

Verification of Measures of Success

If you have read this once, you have read it a dozen times: Verification deliverables and expectations of the project are critical. During this phase, the focus should be on measurement systems. This is because the effort has now taken on the characteristics of a standard project; oftentimes additional measures of success may come into play.

Be on your guard with measures. In the "delivery of a specific change" project, traditional measures may or may not come into play. Hopefully these process measures and those of success were identified previously, but they may not have been important—until now. Normal project management standards of success include:

- Time – Achievement of intermediate project milestones and ultimately the required date of change (project closure)

- Cost – Not exceeding any of the identified costs related to the project. This includes both monetary and non-monetary costs

- Scope – Achieving the expected changes, to the expected "process population" with the expected impact

Many traditional project management "schools" teach that there is a fourth measure of success. That measure is quality. That would bring a traditional project exactly into the previously mentioned TVQC measurements. However, the aforementioned PM Lite course is based upon a modification to the traditionally accepted Project Triangle. It is represented in the following diagram:

The PM Lite methodology holds that the quality of project delivery is dependent on the performance to the previously mentioned factors. If these are clearly defined and monitored, then the quality is a foregone conclusion. From a PM Lite perspective, measuring delivery quality is a non-value added effort. The characteristics driving a project's quality are embedded within the other three characteristics. This is simply a matter of semantics, and it is not worth the time or effort to argue this matter. If a fourth measure is required by the organization, include it.

In traditional projects, the killer characteristic to control is the project's scope. Many a project has become a career because of additions and changes. Some interesting characteristics that become apparent as the comprehensive project plan for a DMADD project is developed. The relentless emphasis on the delivery requirements and exit strategy make the project's scope almost a null point. It is clearly documented what is expected of the project and its goals. Scopes seldom creep!

In addition, the costs are clearly detailed. As a result, the only characteristic that requires attention is the time element of the project. This is a project manager's dream. The time characteristic, however is what drives risk in the project. That is the reason for concerted focus on realistic time lines and project delivery controls. The sponsor and the team leaders must work together to ensure that every milestone is achieved. As a result, risk is mitigated.

New Process Documentation

Running concurrently with the development of the project plan should be the development of the new process' materials. These should include:

- SIPOC
- Process Map
- Standard Operating Procedures (SOPs)
- Service Level Agreements (SLAs)
- Performance Dashboards
- Failure Modes Effects Analysis (FMEA)
- Control Plans

Since the SIPOC and the process map were addresses in the previous phase, we'll forego explanations of those except for the matter of verification. All of the other documents are traditional process documentation tools and any process improvement practitioner should be adept in their development and use. We will not spend much time on the criticality of them. In actuality, the first five tools have been populated for the existing process, in an earlier phase within this project. Unless the project has totally re-engineered the process, these documents will simply be altered.

FMEA

Only two documents have yet to be addressed in detail. They are the failure modes effects analysis (FMEA) and process control plans. I call the FMEA the "I told you so!" tool. The purpose of a good FMEA is to capture and address remaining process risk. This should not be confused with project risk, yet it often is. The new FMEA should capture all of the outstanding risk that is not addressed by the current project. Through the utilization of the C/E/I analysis and the new documentation, the FMEA effort should be relatively simple. In short, it sets the stage for future projects within the project's process, by identifying those elements that the current project has not addressed. During DMADD training, an interesting logical possibility exercise is taught. This actually pre-populates the FMEA and makes the exercise much easier than it traditionally is assembled.

Control Plans

The control plan is often a misunderstood document. It is a natural off-shoot of the FMEA. When a risk can not be totally eliminated through mechanical or technological means, it establishes the responses required. In part it is a thorough standard operating procedure, only with more. It should provide the process owner with a recommended set of controls and responses for those issues that are still expected to arise after the new process is in place. It should also predict the frequency of occurrence. When forecasts are made, the process owner can then compare reality with the projection and then update the FMEA accordingly.

There is an important reason for developing the process documentation at this point in the project. It augments the project plan. Oftentimes, differences between the existing process and the anticipated process become apparent and assist the need for change. One can see that the development of new process documentation activity is not standalone. What is learned from it, especially when it is compared to the current documentation, can help ensure a more comprehensive project plan and drives the project success.

The "Soft-Side" of the Project Plan

Before closing this chapter, we must note that in traditional project plans the people side is often neglected. DMADD recognizes the critical nature of involving all of the right people in the right ways. The soft side is often the hardest part of any project and as a result avoided. The change triad was discussed earlier in this book. At this point, a separate "triad" should be developed for the delivery plan itself. Specificity is critical.

The triad is important, but of greatest significance is the training plan. Any change in the status quo must have a training plan. A change is defined as "any difference in the existing process or technology and the proposed system." The only exception is when something is totally eliminated. That situation is only communicated.

EPO Update

As previously noted, the update and review of the EPO with the sponsor and pertinent decision-makers is an important milestone in every phase. At this stage, the review will be significantly more time consuming. The primary reason is that the project plan should be reviewed in excruciating detail and updated by the input received from the reviewers. The goal of the EPO and plan review is to obtain full approval and support to go ahead with the implementation of the recommendation from the analyze phase. Once this approval is obtained, the project should kick the project communication plan into high gear, along with the actual activity plan. It is time to move into the last stage.

119

Chapter 8

DMADD – Deliver

DELIVERABLES:

1. Final Pilot and Approval
2. Delivery of Solution
3. Verification of Performance
4. Handoff
5. Lessons Learned
6. Executive Project Overview (EPO)

PHASE GOALS:

- Final Pilot and Approval to Finalize Delivery of Solution
- Verification of Sustained Results
- Full Handoff of Process to Process Owners
- Finalization and Review of Lessons Learned
- Transfer of Lessons Learned to Knowledge Manager
- Final Project Review and Exit

The bottom-line of this phase is providing the expected results! All of the work of the prior stages, the comprehensive documentation and activity in the world is of little value if it is not focused on delivering the expected goals. The develop stage ensures that focus is developed and maintained.

All of the heavy lifting has been accomplished during the prior four phases within DMADD. The delivery phase focuses on the elements of the aforementioned project triangle. With scope and cost controlled by other DMADD tools, the primary concern of the project manager or DMADD project leader is time. DMADD leverages the best tools of project management to support the successful delivery. The selection and support of an expert project manager is also critical. Do not trust critical projects to novices.

During the development of the project, the ADS, inter-relationship diagram and WBS established the details of the required changes to people, process and technology. These were then captured in an (organizational standard) project plan.

During the course of the project, the plan and its pictorial (Gantt) representation are continuously updated and regularly reported to the stakeholders. The reporting format is a PM Lite-specific tool called ISA. ISA stands for issues/stopgaps/adjustments. All reporting should focus on items on this report. Expensive executive time is wasted on project leaders reporting item by item that they are on track. Sponsors and decision-makers should be keenly aware of every item that is or may be a risk to delivering the project on time.

Final Pilot and Final Approval

In the previous stage, a small pilot confirmed the information provided by the model. This helped finalize the decision to go. It still may be the case that the organization does not fully trust the project's recommendation. The argument for the change was sufficiently compelling to warrant a pilot or a test but not a full implementation. Many practitioners take the need for a pilot as an insult or a show of distrust. A pilot is not an indicator of a project's weakness or a lack of organizational trust and support. It is often a wise business decision and a confirmation or information-gathering technique. The pilot in this stage is not the same as the previous pilot and probably not what traditional process improvement professionals would call a pilot. Let's dig deeper and find the differences.

This pilot is more a case of project timing than it is a small-scale trial run (like the previous pilot). It is really the finalized changes to the process with the old bridges still intact. If this pilot does not provide the expected results, the old system remains intact and the project can be reversed and reattempted with the lessons learned.

The real change occurs when it operates as expected and the old system goes away. Then the project not only finalizes the project changes but the definition of "change" licenses the project to eliminate any opportunities for reverting back to the "old way" of doing things. One of the means by which DMADD effects sustained change is by burning the bridges. Then individuals within the process can not run back to the old way.

Pilots, traditionally, have been conducted to test theories. Scientific method has had undue influence on organizational process piloting. As a result, pilots are often conducted in a hands-off venue. In DMADD, process piloting focuses upon the achievement of the project requirements at any cost. Then results are then compared not at the output performance level, but at the cost associated with the achievement (input requirements). This provides a final go/no-go decision point.

Pilot reviews are relatively simple and the associated documentation follows suit. The following document has been effectively utilized in pilot reviews, in past projects:

Philip C. Reinke

Pilot Review

Performance Characteristic	Required Performance	Pilot Performance	Achieved (Y/N)	Time Required	Volume Required	Cost Required	Acceptable (Y/N)

Overall Pilot Performance Acceptable?   (Y/N)   if No, What changes are required? _____

Pilot Continuation Approved?   (Y/N) if No, What are the reasons for discontinuation? _____

Sponsor _____ Date _____

This document consolidates all of the required "whats," "how much's," and "costs." The decision related to acceptance is then reduced to this question: "Are we willing to pay the cost associated to achieve the required results?" It is simply a matter of make this new way of doing things permanent.

For the sake of this discussion, let's assume that the pilot performed as expected, the associated costs of performance was within organizational reason (budget) and the full implementation (burning the bridges) was approved. In actuality, if the project is given the correct amount of support and the leader/team does their work, approval is commonplace. In fact, project abandonment at this stage is a rarity. It is time to put the delivery system in gear and drive to completion!

Delivery of the Solution

The actual project management methodology that is utilized at this point is somewhat irrelevant. DMADD can adapt to any generally accepted methodology as long as it has these two components:
- A detailed project plan
- A standardized reporting system

124

An organization should not get caught up in a "format war." Work lists, indented subordinate projects, contingency plans, etc. are irrelevant and simply a matter of personal preference. Whatever works for an organization and delivers results, works for DMADD. The heavy lifting has already been done and the stage for success set.

Without belaboring the point, let's assume that the organizationally accepted project plan is executed and the full implementation project begins.

ISA Project Status Communication

One of the major shortcomings that I have encountered across nearly all of the organizations that I have worked with was project status communication. Inordinate amounts of expensive executive time was wasted listening to project leaders avoiding the "bad news" or laying a foundation for the letdown or making excuses for falling short of expectations. This list could be nearly endless.

ISA (pronounced "ee-sah") helps add value to project updates. The purpose of a project review is to keep a project on track. The attendees of the update meeting are there to lend assistance to the project leader and the team, when their efforts are not effective. ISA keeps the meeting focused on the issues at hand and engages the meeting participants on rectifying the issues and roadblocks. The document used in an ISA meeting drives the meeting towards action. How?

- If there are no issues on ISA, the meeting is not conducted.

- There is no room on the document for any areas that are operating as expected. It must be assumed by the meeting participants that if it is not on the ISA, it is OK.

- It specifically identifies the issue (which may be hyperlinked to more detail).

- It requires a stopgap effort (which may be hyper-linked to more detail).

- It requires the project leader to assess the project for the impact and the required adjustment.

- It requires a recommendation to either be present at the meeting or one should be created prior to the close of the meeting.

- It requires authorization to move forward.

The following document has been effectively utilized in past projects in ISA meetings:

	Issue	Impact	Stop-Gap	Adjustment	Recommendation	Approval
1						
2						
3						
4						
5						
6						
7						

As you think through ISA, you probably said to yourself, "I wish all of my meetings were like this." As a matter of fact, ISA is one of the management tools that we teach and utilize broadly across organizations. Our saying has become, "ISA is not just for projects anymore!" An organization would be well-served if its people (especially it management) made ISA-type discussions a standard discussion rather than a rare event.

For the sake of the overall discussion, let's now assume that the required changes of the project have been delivered, its effectiveness was confirmed, and the bridges were burned. The project leader's exit is at hand. There are a few milestones that must be accomplished in order for the overall effort to be fully successful. They are:

- Re-Verification of Sustained Results
- Handoff to Process Owners
- Lessons Learned - Development and Knowledge Transfer
- Final EPO – (Review and Approval of Exit Strategy)

Verification of Sustained Results

Many projects have failed their overall objectives because the project leaders were quick to jump off the project bandwagon before the changes could be validated as sustained. In DMADD, the shift is considered sustained when it meets the data-run (consecutive data points) according to the corresponding Shewhart rule. This can be more easily explained with the following example:

- The baseline process performance average was 2
- The required process performance average was 4
- The change from 2 to 4 is a 1 sigma (standard deviation) shift

In order for the shift to be considered statistically significant and sustained, a run of eight consecutive data points must be at or beyond the new average of four. The statistical probability of this occurring solely at random is about 5 percent. A sustained shift can be declared and the project leader can then begin the handoff process. DMADD utilizes Stewart's rules because they are generally accepted and can be applied to nearly every measureable need within an organization.

Handoff to Process Owner

Seldom is a process owner unaware and not fully engaged in the events related to a project in their area. More often than not, the handoff is a formality. At minimum, the process owner should attend the final executive project overview and pledge ongoing support of the initiative.

Lessons Learned – Development and Knowledge Transfer

In the upcoming book *The Perfect Machine*, a specific portion of the organization is dedicated to capturing and retaining all important organizational information. Project information is often overlooked in traditional enterprise content management (ECM) environments. We contend that projects especially the DMADD type contains a great amount of information that may be of significant use in the future. Many times ideas and thoughts rejected at the present time may be applicable to a future issue.

Cataloging as much information as possible and the related insights is not only time-saving, it may also retain information that disappears in the dynamics of the internet. Since discoveries are being made all along the length of the project, the wise project leader begins knowledge transfer as soon as the information and insights become available. Then the finalization of knowledge transfer is a minimal task.

Though knowledge capture and transfer is not critical to the success of the individual project, it is important to ongoing organizational success and project efficiency. This is more of an organizational decision, but after much thought, most organizations do pursue this aspect of *The Perfect Machine*.

Final EPO – (Review and Approval of Exit Strategy)

Many projects linger because project leaders and/or organizations do not know how to close and exit. When an effort is successful, seeing it come to a close is a mixed emotional experience. The final EPO is a time for celebration and review. The formal "Well done!" comes when the exit strategy that was created in the beginning of the project is reviewed and the sponsors and decision-makers confirm that all is completed and to their satisfaction.

During the course of this review, insights should be shared and recommendations for future projects discussed. It is often a time to share war stories. This information should be formally documented and retained either by the "Knowledge Manager" or by the sponsor and the project leader.

Many times, a review of the new FMEA is in order. This is

128

a time to review the remaining process risks and what is in place or recommended to be put in place to mitigate these outstanding issues. Many new projects or opportunities come from this discussion.

At this point the project has finally come to a close. An idea has become reality. I have yet to meet a project leader who can simply walk away from that. A good project leader will always have an affinity for that process and is often a great consideration within the organization's progression planning. Within weeks all of the ill feelings, turmoil and roadblocks will have been forgotten. Only a legend survives and that legend ends with a happy ending—whether it was what was originally suggested or something entirely new.

Chapter 9

Making Change Last

UNLESS a project delivers the required results and those results are sustained, the efforts are useless. One of the final activities in the last stage of DMADD during the handoff to the process owners is the confirmation of the sustained performance at the required levels. This helps prove to the mainstream that the new performance levels are possible, and sustaining them is possible. It also helps identify any challengers to the new process (this may be intentional, but most of the time, it is unintentional) and allows the organization to emphasize the need for the new system.

The forthcoming book, *The Perfect Machine* describes a function that independently monitors all processes that have had project influence. This monitoring is ongoing and continuous. It also audits each of these processes on a quarterly basis. Any degradation in the process' performance is immediately addressed. This helps ensure that the new goals are sustained. Lacking this component of the perfect machine, an organization should make ongoing monitoring and reporting a responsibility of the process owner and the quarterly audit the responsibility of the project sponsor.

It is also well advised that any organization considering wide spread use of DMADD develop an internal PI Machine. The Machine (as I loving refer to it) is not a cost center! It often con-

131

tributes more to the organizational bottom-line than many of its revenue generating components. That is a bold statement, but I stand confidently behind it.

More detailed information can be obtained by contacting the Continuous Improvement Institute, on their website: www. thecii.com. The Cii can provide Analytics, Project Support and Training & Certification.

Someone once said, "Only a mad man would attempt to create an improvement methodology applicable to the 21st century" How about a DMADD man? Good luck in your organizational endeavors and challenges—and welcome to the 21st Century!

Chapter 10

What's Next?

DMADD is not intended to be an be-all, end-all methodology. It does, however contain a characteristic that makes it unique among many of the traditional techniques. DMADD, in and of itself, is self-improving. When combined with the knowledge Management component which is detailed in the book *The Perfect Machine*," it is a continuous improvement methodology that is designed to improve itself and adapt to the dynamics of this climate.

What may not be readily apparent is that DMADD, is more than a process improvement methodology. It is the management methodology for the 21st century. We call it CIMM, which stands for continuous improvement management methodology. It is the way that leaders (in fact everyone working in an organization) should think, work, and act. An organization will function as a well-oiled machine, if the majority of its constituents have a DMADD mindset, skill-set and behavior-set. This is not a pipe-dream or an empty promise. I have seen it work!

My career commitment for the past 25 years has been to foster executives of the 21st century. Early in my career I was lucky to have been mentored by an extremely future-sited individual who did that for me. Over the course of the relationship, I learned much from him. Then he set me off on my own. While I studied to become a "professional manager," I observed how effective organizations and successful individuals operated. I noted that an unspoken DMADD was, in one way or another, embedded in their DNA. As I look back at some of the great successes, the road leading to them followed the DMADD route. As an organization or as an organizational leader, I would suggest considering the culture of CIMM combined with DMADD as the way you do business.

I anticipate that organizational needs will change and a new methodology will arise, and someday DMADD will be replaced. DMADD is unique in that it has a chameleon-like nature makes it adaptive to its environment and its ability to identify ever-changing needs will make it applicable for decades to come! As before, I anxiously await the next methodology and desire to see where process and continuous improvement goes.

CPSIA information can be obtained at www.ICGtesting.com
Printed in the USA
LVOW111244261011

252149LV00005B/209/P